FESTOOL® ESSENTIALS

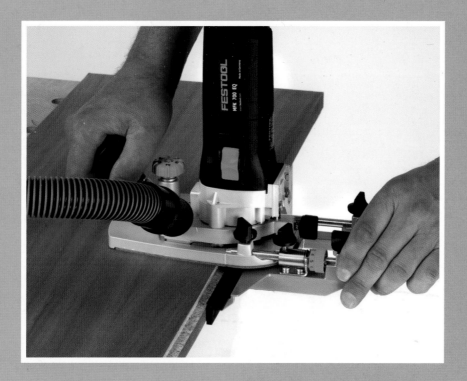

The Routers

- **OF 1010 EQ**
- **OF 1400 EQ**
- **OF 2200 EB**
- **MFK 700 EQ**

Schiffer Publishing Ltd®

4880 Lower Valley Road   Atglen, Pennsylvania 19310

Copyright © 2009 by Schiffer Publishing Ltd.
Library of Congress Control Number: 2009938218

Covers and book designed by: Bruce Waters
Type set in Humanist 521 BT

ISBN: 978-0-7643-3323-1
Printed in China

CONTENTS

INTRODUCTION

The company Albert Fezer and Gottlieb Stoll founded in 1925, in southern Germany, has been known by many names, Fezer & Stoll, Festo, Festo Tooltechnic, and, beginning in 2000, Festool. Whatever the name, the mission has always been the same: to provide expert craftspeople with the finest tools available to make their work more efficient, easier, and better. From the beginning they have committed themselves to understanding the needs of the craftsperson in an ever-changing workplace. They have addressed those needs with innovation, quality, and performance that is unsurpassed in the industry. The result is captured in their three-word credo: "Faster, Easier, Smarter."

Today the name Festool stands for an integrated system of tools engineered for ease of use and reliability, to increase the accuracy, creativity, and productivity of the workplace. Each tool in designed to be used with the powerful dust extraction system, which is covered here in great detail.

Used with Festool routers and saws, the Festool guide and worktable systems allow for unsurpassed accuracy, convenience, and flexibility.

1. THE PORTABLE ROUTERS

The Festool system offers a router for every need. Like all Festool products the four routers in the line represent the highest standards of engineering and quality and are designed with the user's needs in mind. Exacting tolerances and quality materials insure that the Festool routers will provide many years of reliable service.

The Festool line of routers has been designed for a wide variety of uses, from laminate trimming to making heavy cuts in hardwoods, from work with solid surface materials to dovetail joints. All are designed to work efficiently with the dust extraction system and the OF 1010, OF 1400, and OF 2200 are integrated with the guide rail system for accuracy and ease of use when making routing grooves and dados.

Festool Portable Routers

Specifications	OF 1010 EQ	OF 1400 EQ	OF 2200 EB
Power consumption	1010 watts / 8.5 amps 120 v AC	1400 watts / 11.7 amps 120 v AC	2200 watts / 18 amps 120 v AC
Collet diameter range	1/4" and 8 mm	1/4", 1/2", and 8 mm	1/2"
Drive shaft speed	10,000 - 23,000 rpm	10,000 - 22,500 rpm	10,000 - 22,000 rpm
Quick depth adjustment range	2 1/8"	2 3/4"	3 5/32"
Weight	5.94 lbs (2.7 kg)	9.9 lbs. (4.5 kg)	17.2 lbs. (7.8 kg)

Specifications	OF 1010 EQ	OF 1400 EQ	OF 2200 EB
Standard Package Contents			
Collet—1/4"	•	•	
Collet—8mm	•	•	
Collet—1/2"	•	•	
Chip catcher	•	•	•
Dust extraction hood	•	•	•
Guide stop	•		
Standard U.S. guide bushing adapter	•	•	•
Plug-it power cord	•	•	•
Systainer	SYS 3	SYS 4	SYS 4

Accessories

Specifications	OF 1010 EQ	OF 1400 EQ	OF 2200 EB
Clamping Collets			
1/4" (6.35mm) Collet w/Nut	488760	492141	–
1/4" (6.35mm) Clamping Collet	488761	492141	494463
1/2" Collet w/ Nut	–	–	494465
6mm Collet w/Nut	488755	–	–
8mm Collet w/ Nut	488761	–	494460
Edging Guides, Stops, & Circles			
Edge Guide	489427	492636	494680
Edge Stop	485758	485758	–
Edging Plate	486058	486058	–
Guide Stop	488752	492601	–
Guide Rail Base Kit	–	–	494681
Guide Connecting Rods	–	–	495247
Other Accessories			
Angle Arm	486052		–
Base Accessory Kit, *Imperial*	–	–	495249
Base Accessory Kit, *Metric*	–	–	495248
parallel edge guide, guide stop, guide rods, table widener base, small bore base, template guide base, offset base for guide rail, & metric template guide bushings			
Chip Catcher	493180	–	494670
Chip Deflector	486242	–	–
Dust Extraction Hood	–	492585	–
Dust Hood	–	492000	–
Fine Adjustment	488754	–	–
Hard Fiber Base Runner	489229	–	–
Sliding Stop Flag	–	485759	–
Small Bore Base	–	–	494677
Support Foot	–	438608	438608
Table Widener	493139	493233	494682
Template Guides			
Centering Mandrel	492187		
Guide Bushing Adaptor	469625	493566	494627
Template Guide Base		494675	
Template Guide, 1/2" OD		495339	
Template Guide, 3/4" OD		495340	

Template Guide, 1" OD		495341	
Template Guide, 1-3/8" OD		495342	
Template Guide, 8.5mm OD/6.5mm ID		–	
(for VS 600 joining system)	490772	492179	–
Template Guide, 10.8mm OD/9mm ID	486029	–	–
Template Guide, 13.8mm OD/11mm ID	484176	–	–
Template Guide, 13.8mm OD/11mm ID			
(for VS 600 joining system)	–	492180	–
Template Guide, 17mm OD/15mm ID	486030	–	494622
Template Guide, 17mm OD/15mm ID			
(for VS 600 joining system)	490770	492181	–
Template Guide, 24mm OD/21mm ID	486031	492183	494623
Template Guide, 24mm OD/22mm ID		–	
(for VS 600 joining system)	490771	492182	–
Template Guide, 27mm OD/25mm ID	486032	492184	494624
Template Guide, 30MM OD/27mm ID	486033	492185	494625
Template Guide, 40MM OD/37mm ID	486034	492186	494626

Guides and Jigs

Trammel Unit [483922]	•		
Plexiglas® Template Routing Aid [495246]	•	•	•
MFS 400 Multi-Routing Template [492610]	•	•	•
MFS 700 Multi-Routing Template [492611]	•	•	•
Routing Slide [492728]	•	•	•
LR 32 Hole Drilling Set [583290]	•	•	•
32mm Hole Drilling Guide, 1080mm [491621]	•	•	
32mm Hole Drilling Guide, 2424mm [491622]	•	•	
VS 600 Joining System [488876]	•	•	

Note: Item numbers are subject to change. Check with Festool USA for the latest offerings.

OF 1010 EQ

OF 1010 EQ

The smallest of the Festool general-purpose routers, the OF 1010 EQ is a powerful, versatile tool for precise work. Its ergonomic design permits easy one-handed operation, allowing the operator to switch it on and off, plunge, cut, and release with ease, while its size permits extended periods of work without fatigue. Lightweight and compact, it is balanced to provide great maneuverability, with enough power to handle all 1/4" and 8mm bits. Micro-adjustments to 1/256" (0.1 mm) permit extreme accuracy.

Specifications

Collet Diameter Range:	1/4" and 8mm
Drive shaft speed:	10,000 - 23,000 rpm
Power Consumption:	1010 watts/8.5 amps
	120 v AC
Quick depth adjustment range:	2 3/16" (55mm)
Weight:	5.94 lbs (2.7 kg)

Includes

Chip catcher	●
Collet—1/4"	●
Collet—8mm	●
Dust extraction hood	●
Guide stop	●
Plug-it power cord	●
Standard U.S. guide bushing adapter	●
Systainer	SYS 3

PERFORMANCE

• **MMC (Multiple Material Controls) Electronics.** Equipped with electronic controls, Festool routers maintain constant speed under load, improving cut quality. MMC electronics also allow for step-less variable speed for different applications, and overload protection for longer life.

• **Versatility & Power.** The lightness of the OF 1010 EQ, less than 6 lbs., makes it easily maneuverable for most common routing tasks. Its power, at 1010 watts, is sufficient for most tasks.

PRECISION

• **Precision Depth Adjustment.** With micro-adjustability to 1/256" (0.1 mm) it is possible to obtain tremendous precision while routing.

• **Depth Turret.** Three-position, adjustable depth stop turret for repeatable and consistent step cutting.

• **Central Column Clamp.** Securely holds the plunge depth for two-handed routing and easily released with a twist.

EASE OF USE

• **Ergonomic Handle.** The full-grip handle allows precise control while reducing fatigue. The variable speed control is integrated into the handle at the thumb position, allowing for one-handed operation.

• **Auxiliary Handle.** The additional handle at the front of the motor casing allows for two-handed control.

• **Switch Lock.** The power switch locks on, so control can be maintained from a variety of grip positions.

• **Quad Center Line Marks.** The OF 1010 EQ has a center line indention on each side of the base, providing a visual reference point for aligning the center of the bit with the cut line.

• **Plunge Action.** The smooth 2-1/8" plunge action provides complete control. A twist of the auxiliary handle locks the router in the plunge position.

WORK FLOW

• **Dust Extraction.** Like all Festool power tools, the OF 1010 EQ is integrated with the dust extraction system, taking the dust and debris from around the bit so visibility is increased and clean-up time is nearly eliminated. The port is designed so that the hose and the power cord are parallel, avoiding the awkward tangle that occurs with some other routers.

• **Plug-It Power Cord.** The power cords on the routers are the same as most other Festool tools, allowing a fast, efficient changeover between tools and enhancing the workflow. And they are 13 feet long.

• **System Integration.** Designed to be used with a complete line of Festool guides and jigs, including the FS guide rail system for guided cutting, VS 600 Dovetail jig for joinery applications, LR32 hole drilling system, MFS multi-routing templates, and a wide range of other accessory options.

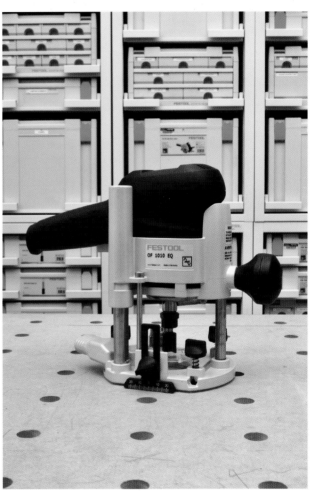

The overall view of the OF 1010.

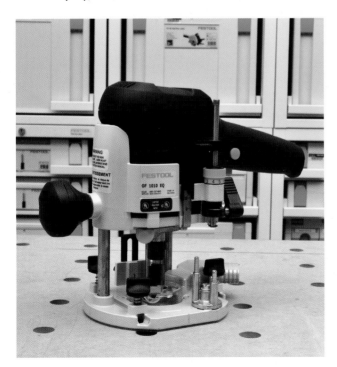

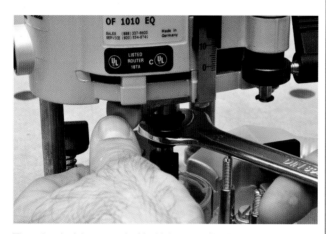

The arbor lock is engaged with this button, allowing one-wrench bit changes.

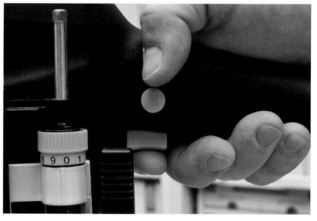

The on/off switch and lock are designed for easy use.

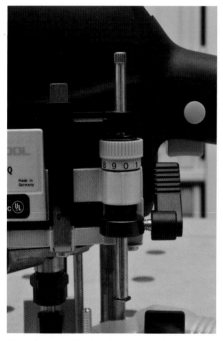

This precision depth adjuster has micro capabilities, with each number representing 0.1mm (1/256")

The variable speed control dial.

All routers are equipped with Multiple Material Controls (MMC). This electronic component provides for variable speed, soft start, circuit overload protection, thermal overload protection, and constant speed under load.

This support keeps the route[...] [...]ce dust shroud works in conjunction with the dust extrac-
rail. The scale is centered with [...] [...]n for the efficient removal of waste material.
starting and stopping points of [...]
example, when making a blind [...]

The housing is also marked on all four si[...] [...]rt is designed to easily fit around the bit and to
the router bit. Again, the center line is us[...] [...]tting area. It has a center opening of 25mm,
making it easier and faster. [...] [...]when larger bits are used.

The three-position depth stop turret. [...] rear.

OF 1010 EQ

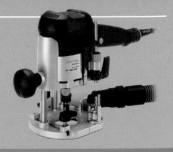

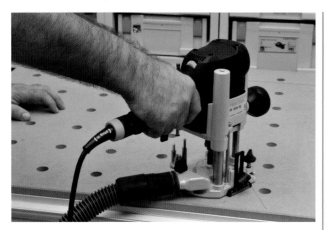

The dust extraction hose and power cord are in alignment, helping to keep them out of the way when routing.

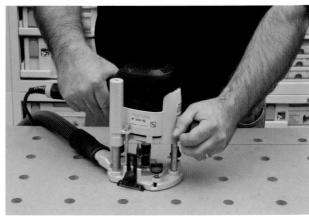

All the controls and the column locking knob are within easy reach.

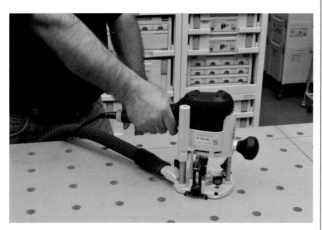

The OF 1010 EQ is equipped with a long handle for one-handed operation.

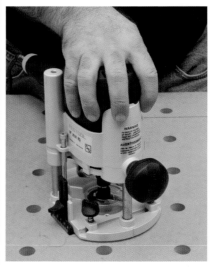

The OF 1010 EQ can also be easily held from the top.

It also has a second knob on the front that can be used in two-handed operations. It doubles as the column locking knob.

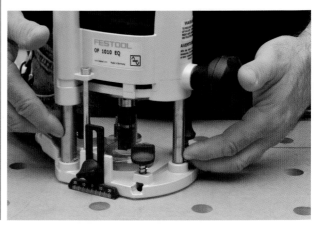

There are two depth columns to eliminate play.

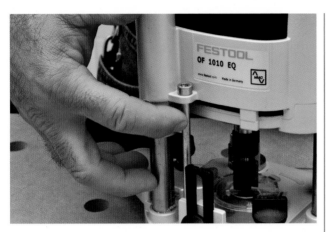

The column stop rod keeps the router attached to the base.

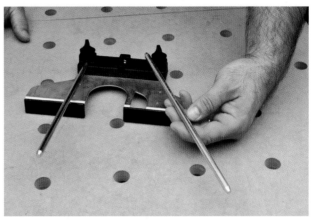

The guide accessories connect to the router with rods.

The plate is made of a phenolic resin. It slides easily and is resistant to deep scratches. Because of this, it is less likely to pick up debris that will scratch your work.

The parallel edge guide is a basic optional accessory. Insert the rods in the slots and tighten…

The black ring is removable so accessories can be installed.

…then insert it into the slots of the router.

Use the scribe line to align the router and lock the parallel edge guide in position with the three knobs.

The result.

Plunge the router to the correct depth…

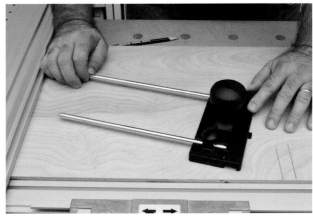

The guide stop accessory integrates the router with the Festool guide rail system. The rods are inserted completely into the guide stop and tightened.

…and cut the groove.

The guide stop should ride smoothly on the rail with no play. Check the fit and make any necessary adjustments.

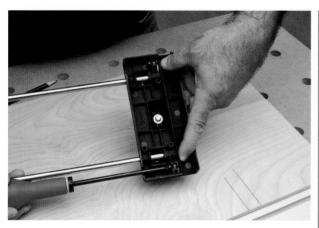

The guide rail tolerance is adjusted with two set screws on the underside.

To set the support, hold the guide stop down so it properly engages the rail, lower the support until it touch the surface, then lock it in place.

When the guide stop is properly adjusted to the guide rail, run the rods into the base plate of the router.

Centering a dado cut is often done by drawing the edges of the cut and aligning the bit with the marks.

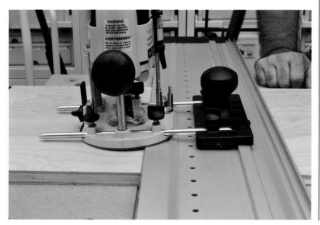

The foot of the router should be partially supported by the guide rail; the amount of overlap varies, depending on the cut. As seen here, the router will have a tendency to tilt until the support is engaged.

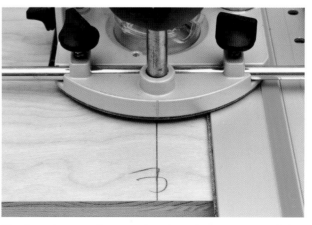

The Festool system offers a much easier and more accurate solution. You simply draw the center line and align the center mark molded into the foot plate with the line.

For the highest level of accuracy, a micro-adjuster is available as an accessory. Attach it to the rod by removing the front foot plate knob nearest the end of the rod…

…and tighten the knob on the adjuster.

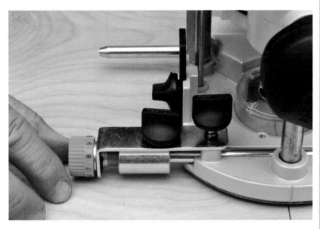

…and sliding the micro-adjuster onto the end of the rod. Replace the knob.

The green knob can now be used to micro-adjust to the line. As with the micro-adjustment on the router, each whole number is 0.1 mm. When the center alignment is accurately set, retighten all knobs.

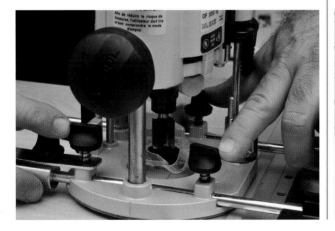

To use the micro-adjuster, loosen the three foot plate knobs…

Setting the depth begins by pushing the router down until the bit touches the material and locking it in place with the column lock knob at the front.

Turn the three depth stop turret so the lowest screw is under the depth rod.

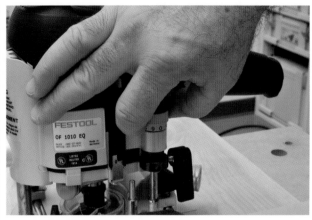

Zero out the green micro-adjuster.

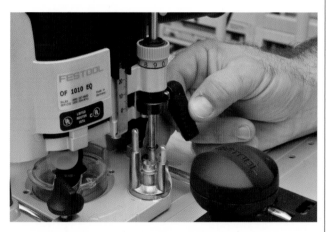

Loosen the depth rod locking lever and lower the depth rod so it touches the turret screw.

Now lift the depth rod to the desire depth, using the depth scale.

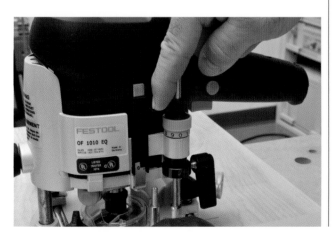

If necessary, slide the black plastic depth scale to zero.

Engage the lever to lock it in place.

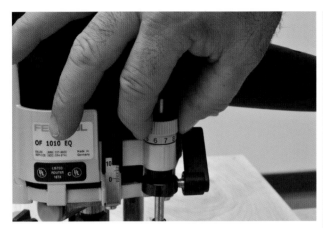

Fine tuning is done with the micro-adjuster. Turning it counterclockwise (going down in numbers) makes the depth shallower, each number being 0.1mm

As before, disengage the depth gauge locking lever…

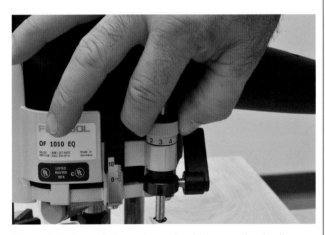

Turning it clockwise (going up in numbers) increases the depth.

…and zero out the depth scale…

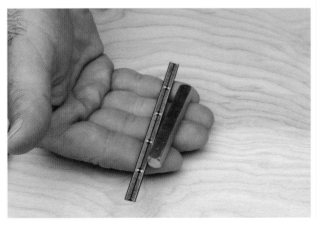

A faster and easier alternative is to use the material itself or a gauge block to set the depth.

Lift the depth gauge rod…

...and insert the gauge block or material on the top of the turret screw. Lower the rod to touch...

Remove the inlay and turn the micro-adjuster down, creating a shallower cut, which will leave the inlay proud of the surface.

...and lock in place.

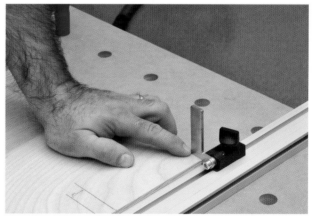

If you are doing opposite sides of a cabinet like a bookcase, once you have the set-up complete, it is useful to use a stop flag on the guide rail to allow for a repetitive cut.

Inlay should be a little proud of the surface. To do this set the gauge as before to the thickness of the inlay and lock in place.

When the router is correctly aligned, plunge into the cut...

...and move along the guide rail.

Sometimes, because of variations in the material, the joint can be a bit tight. The stop flag on the guide rail is useful in correcting this.

For deeper cuts it is sometimes advisable to make multiple passes, a process that is made easy with the guide rail system.

Simply insert a business card or similar paper between the stop flag on the MFT fence and the end of the board as shim stock.

The result.

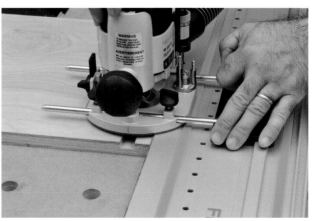

This will move the stock just slightly, so that a second dado cut will widen the cut by the thickness of the shim.

The result. This can also be done with the micro-adjuster, the thickness of the card being about 0.3mm. Be sure to remove the paper or return the micro-adjuster to zero before making a repetitive cut.

Loosen the collar.

BIT CHANGES

Before making any tooling change, unplug the machine from the power source. To remove the old bit, the hole in the arbor, seen here, needs to be aligned with the arbor lock by rotating the bit.

A Festool bit has a depth setting line on its shaft that indicates how deeply it should be inserted into the chuck.

Engage the arbor lock.

Insert the bit to the line…

...and tighten.

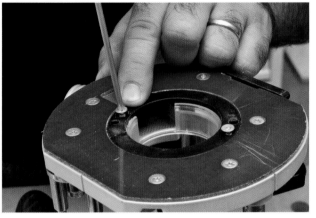

In preparation for installing the rotating chip catcher, remove the black ring from the plate. No.15 torque screws hold it in place.

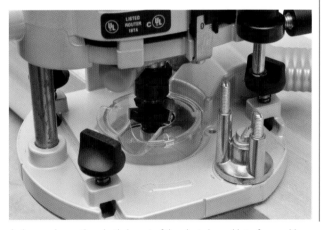

As is seen here, the plastic insert of the dust shroud interferes with a profile bit and needs to be removed.

Place the chip catcher in the plate so the tab fits in the slot and screw in place. The chip catcher is designed to impede the chip from flying off so it can be drawn into the CT dust extractor.

PROFILE WORK WITH THE OF 1040 EQ

Profile work with the OF 1040 EQ requires that a chip catcher, like the one on the left, be installed.

For optimal control, the router should be held at a 30 degree angle to the material when being used.

The adapter will hold most two-part template guides.

The chip collector rotates and should be in this position relative to the wood while routing.

Loosely install the template guide into the adapter.

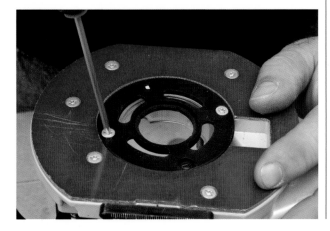

TEMPLATE GUIDES

When using the router with templates, first install the universal template guide adapter, using the two screws from the black plate ring.

The Festool centering mandrel has been designed with a shank that has both 1/4 inch and 1/8 inch diameters, to accommodate both types of bits.

Insert the mandrel through the template guide and into the collar. This will center the template guide. When centered, tighten the guide.

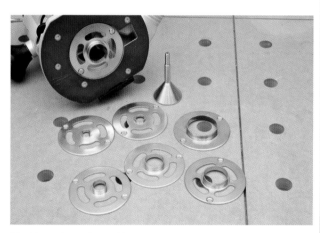

The Festool template guides come in seven sizes, ranging from 10.8mm to 40mm O.D.

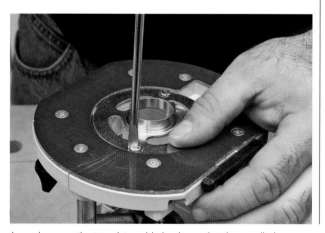

Loosely screw the template guide in place using the supplied slotted screws.

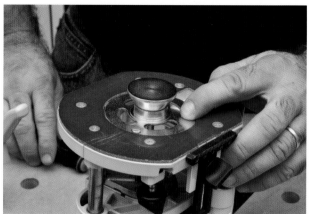

Insert the center mandrel through the guide and into the collar, centering the template guide.

Tighten the screws.

The guide runs along the template. There will always be an offset from the template to the bit. This offset can be determined mathematically with the following formula.

$$\frac{\text{(O.D. of the template guide)} - \text{(diam. of the bit)}}{2}$$

For example: if the O.D. of the template guide is 30 mm and the bit is 18 mm in diameter the offset is 30 minus 18, or 12, divided by 2 for an offset of 6mm. Fractions are harder, but a 3/4 inch template guide and a bit that is 1/2 inch diameter would mean 3/4 minus 1/2, or 1/4, divided by 2, resulting in an offset of 1/8 inch. This formula applies to the template guides for all routers.

ACCESSORIES AND ATTACHMENTS

OF 1010 Table Widener

The OF 1010 Table Widener increases the surface area of the sub-base and comes with a chip catcher held on by three magnets. It provides added support when using a large diameter bit for profiling

To install, first remove the standard sub-base.

...and install the table widener.

Next remove the support...

The larger base gives much more router support and increases control, especially when using a large bit.

OF 1010 EQ

Extension Table

The Extension Table increases the area of the sub-base. The diameter of the hole is 13mm, but can be plunged through, creating a zero clearance opening.

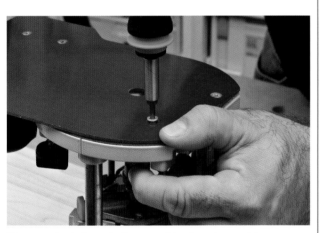

The extender bolts to the bottom of the face plate, so it is not adjustable. The rods on the top give it rigidity.

Added to the standard sub-base, it increases the surface area of the base plate and adds an auxiliary hand hold for increased stability.

Flush Trimming Accessories

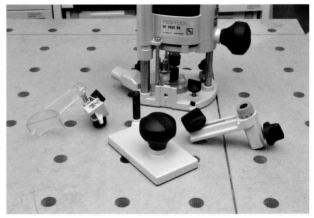

For horizontal flush trimming operations you need these accessories (l-r): chip deflector, edging plate, and angle arm.

With the standard sub-base in place, remove the support.

Install the angle arm in place of the support.

The edging plate has a threaded post.

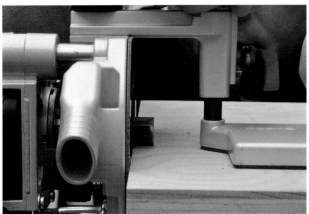

Here it is a little proud.

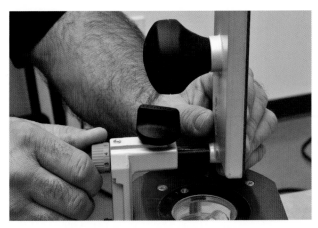

Screw the angle arm into the edging plate by turning the green knob clockwise until it is well engaged.

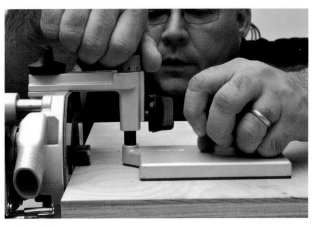

Use the micro-adjuster for the proper fit...

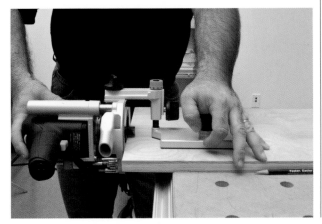

On a surface, with the bit in the plunged position and locked, turn the bit so one blade is at its lowest position. The goal is to adjust the position of the router so the bit touches the surface without cutting into it.

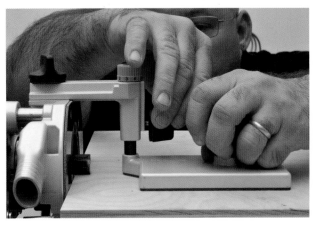

...and lock it in place with the black knob.

Now adjust the plunge depth to the thickness of the trim, but a little proud. Lock it in place.

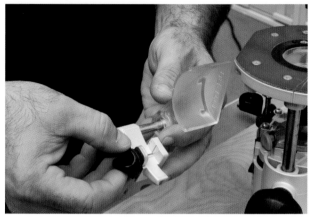

The chip deflector helps direct waste into the dust extraction system.

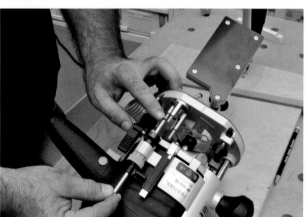

Set the depth gauge to the shortest turret…

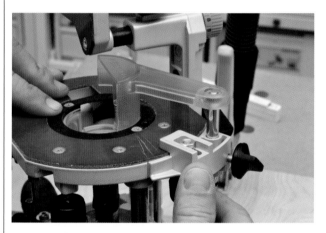

The chip deflector fits inside the black ring and its support attaches to the base plate. The edge will align with the center mark. Lock it in place.

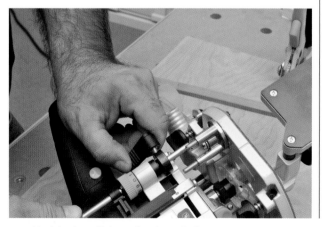

…and lock in place. Release the plunge lock.

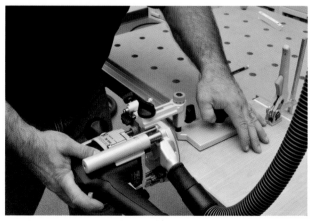

In this configuration, the router is pulled toward you. Make a test pass…

..and check for flushness. After micro-adjustments, you should be ready to trim the edge.

Screw the bearing into place. The bearing should be approximately the diameter of the bit you are using and should be set in the angle arm so it is even with the cutting edge of the bit.

Copier Scanning

The copier scanning set works with the angle arm to copy templates. It comes with a rod and three bearings.

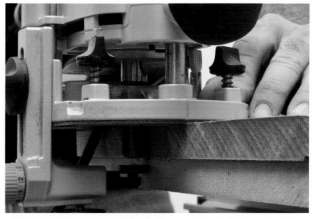

The piece to be copied is positioned under the work piece and slightly recessed, so we can flush fit the work piece to it. The bit should be plunged to match the depth of the work piece.

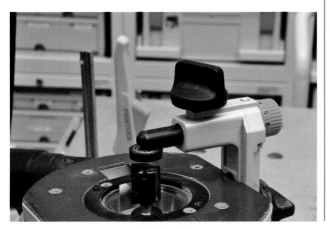

The rod screws into the angle arm by turning the green micro-adjuster knob, and the bearing screws into the rod. Their position is secured with the black knob. The micro-adjuster knob is then used for fine tuning the setting.

The work piece is trimmed as the bearing runs along the template beneath.

OF 1400 EQ

The highly versatile OF 1400 Router lends itself to the multiple demands of the tradesperson. At 1400 watts of power it is strong enough for most routing tasks. Weighing in at 9.9 lbs. it is light enough to be very maneuverable. It can use 1/2", 1/4" or 8 mm bits. Its 2-3/4" plunge depth makes it the best in its category, while its precision to 1/256" (0.1 mm) gives it the accuracy needed for the most demanding tasks. Like all Festool products its design is integrated with the dust extraction system, guides, and jigs, making it easy to use while maintaining high levels of efficiency and accuracy.

Includes

Chip catcher	•
Collet—1/2"	•
Collet—1/4"	•
Collet—8mm	•
Dust extraction hood	•
Plug-it power cord	•
Standard U.S. guide bushing adapter	•
Systainer	SYS 4

Specifications

Collet diameter range	1/4", 1/2", and 8 mm
Drive shaft speed	10,000 - 22,500 rpm
Power consumption	1400 watts / 11.7 amps
	120 v AC
Quick depth adjustment range	2 3/4"
Weight	9.9 lbs.

PERFORMANCE

• **MMC Electronics.** Equipped with electronic controls, Festool routers maintain constant speed under load, improving cut quality. MMC electronics also allows for step-less variable speed for different applications, and overload protection for longer life.

• **Versatility & Power.** The lightness of the OF 1400 EQ, less than 6 lbs., makes it easily maneuverable for most common routing tasks. Its power, at 1010 watts, is sufficient for most tasks.

PRECISION

• **Precision Depth Adjustment.** With micro-adjustability to 1/256" (0.1 mm) it is possible to obtain tremendous precision while routing. There are indents at each 0.1 mm increment.

• **Depth Turret.** Three-position, adjustable depth stop turret for repeatable and consistent step cutting.

• **Double Column Clamping.** One knob securely locks the plunge depth, providing less motor to plate deflection.

EASE OF USE

• **Ratcheting Spindle.** A one-wrench, ratcheting design makes bit changes faster and easier.

• **Ergonomic Handle.** The full-grip handle allows precise control while reducing fatigue. The variable speed control is integrated into the handle at the thumb position, allowing for one-handed operation.

• **Auxiliary Handle.** The additional handle at the front of the motor casing allows for two-handed control.

• **Switch Lock.** The power switch locks on, so control can be maintained from a variety of grip positions.

• **Quad Center Line Marks.** The OF 1400 EQ has a center line indention on each side of the base, providing a visual reference point for aligning the center of the bit with the cut line.

• **2-3/4 Plunge Depth.** The deep, 2-3/4" plunge of the OF 1400 EQ is a useful feature for working with templates.

• **Tool-Less Inserts. The self-centering** template guide bushings and the swiveling chip deflector can be attached and removed without tools.

WORK FLOW

• **Swiveling Chip Deflector.** The chip deflector, which comes with the router, can be used with edge forming bits. It provides excellent chip and dust extraction around curves and corners.

• **Dust Extraction.** Like all Festool power tools, the OF 1400 EQ is integrated with the dust extraction system, taking the dust and debris from around the bit so visibility is increased and clean-up time is nearly eliminated. The port is designed so that the hose and the power cord are parallel, avoiding the awkward tangle that occurs with some other routers.

• **Plug-It Power Cord.** The power cords on the routers are the same as most other Festool tools, allowing a fast, efficient changeover between tools and enhancing the workflow.

• **System Integration.** Designed to be used with a complete line of Festool guides and jigs, including the FS guide rail system for guided cutting, VS 600 Dovetail jig for joinery applications, LR32 hole drilling system, MFS multirouting templates, and a wide range of other accessory options.

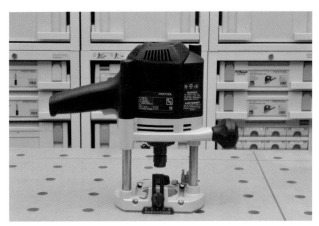

An overview of the OF 1400 EQ.

The spindle switch controls the direction of the ratcheting action. It is clearly marked.

The trigger, trigger lock, and variable speed control are at the back handle and designed for one-handed operation.

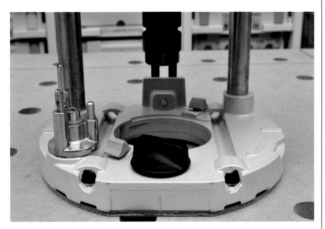

The black knob tightens the two accessory rods. At the left is the three-position depth turret. The green buttons release plate inserts.

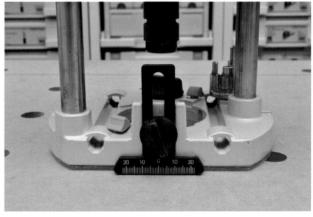

The support

The depth gauge, lock lever, and micro-adjuster are located at the front of the motor casing. The black knob on the left locks the dual columns.

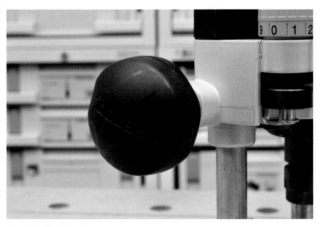

The locking knob

The OF 1400 is designed for tool-less inserts, which simply snap into place.

Like the OF 1010 EQ, the depth adjustment uses the turret, the lock lever, micro-adjuster, and depth gauge.

The OF 1400 has a ratcheting spindle, allowing one wrench bit changes. Engaging the left spindle switch allows a ratcheting wrench action for mounting a bit….

The front knob engages dual locking columns, providing great stability.

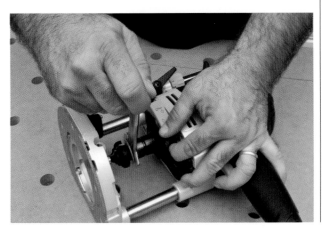

…and engaging the right switch permits the ratcheting wrench action to release the bit.

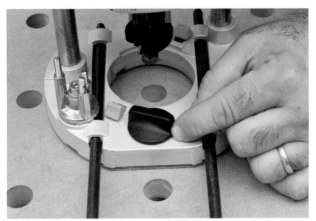

The rods are tightened with a single knob.

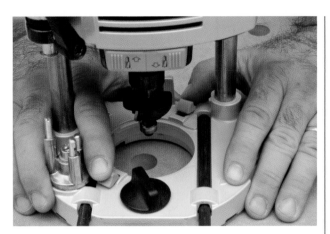

These green buttons are tab releases for plate inserts.

Notice the two tabs at the front. These go into the base plate.

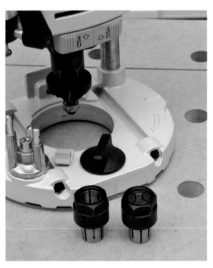

With these adapters, the OF 1400 will accommodate 3 collet sizes, 8mm (installed), 1/4 inch, and 1/2 inch.

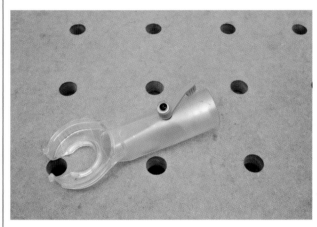

A locking lever is on the underside.

The dust shroud is easily removable.

When the shroud is positioned, the plastic "door" pivots into place to close the circuit. Again, notice the tabs at the lower front edge.

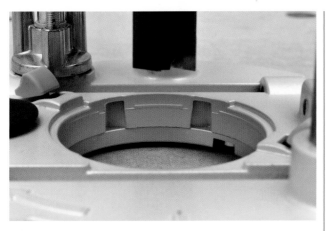

The tabs fit into the two slots in the inner ring of the base plate.

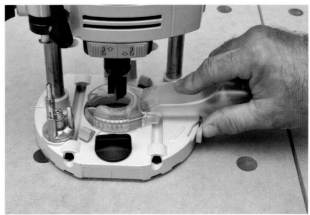

Drop the shroud into place and lock.

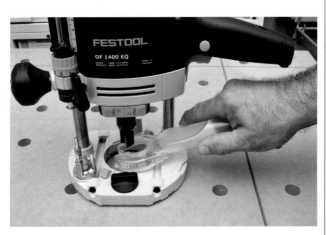

The dust shroud goes in under the handle.

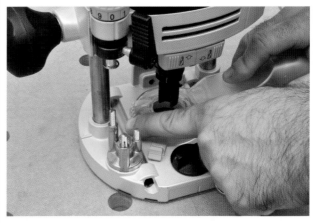

Close the door.

Engage the tabs in the slots.

The dust shroud also works with a large profile bit, which is important because it produces a lot of waste material. Its installation requires an extra step, because the opening in the shroud is smaller than some profile bits.

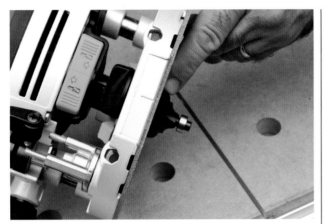

For profile bits, before installing the shroud, plunge the bit to its final working position and lock it in place.

With the bit in its plunged position, rotate the arbor so that the flat surfaces align with the dust shroud and install as before.

The top of the arbor shaft has two flat surfaces…

Lock the dust shroud in place. Remember to remove the dust shroud before releasing the arbor from the plunged position. When you forget to do this, remember that spare dust shrouds are available from Festool.

…that match the front opening of the shroud.

The dust shroud will accommodate a 26 or 37mm hose, but for the OF 1400 the 37mm optimizes dust extraction.

Accessories & Attachments

Chip Catcher

As with the OF 1010, the profile bit needs a chip catcher for effective dust extraction. One of the features of the OF 1400 is that the insert simply snaps into place. The catcher has two tabs on its underside…

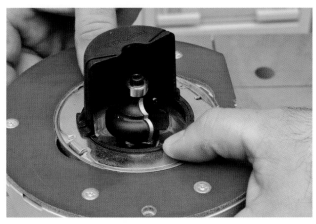

…that slip into slots on the plate and snap into the base. This chip catcher has an opening of 2", and will not accommodate a bit larger than that.

Table Widener

The table widener comes with its own chip collector, held in place with three magnets. In addition to allowing for a larger bit, the table widener creates a more stable surface.

Template Guide Adapters

The universal template guide adapter is self-centering.

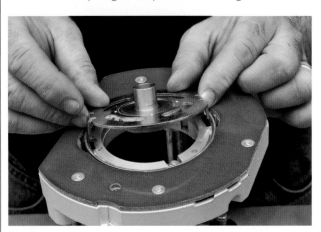

Attach the template guide to the adapter and snap it in place using the tabs

For bits from 2" to 2-1/2" you can switch the base plate to a table widener. As with the OF 1010, simply remove the standard plate and screw the table widener into place, using the screws provided.

The tab design eliminates the need for manual centering.

The micro-adjuster provides fine tuning and the large knob locks the guide in place.

In addition to the universal adapter, 24, 27, 30, and 40mm template guides are available as accessories.

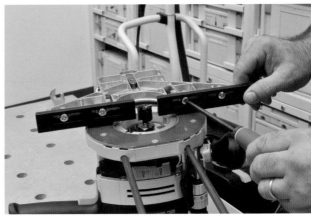

The two-piece composite fence is adjustable, allowing for zero tolerance clearance around the bit. In general the two pieces should be as close to each other as the application allows.

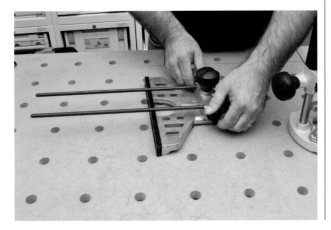

Parallel Edge Guide
The parallel edge guide for the OF 1400 uses rods which are inserted into the guide and locked.

A dust shroud is included with the edge guide, providing collection from below.

The parallel edge guide installed.

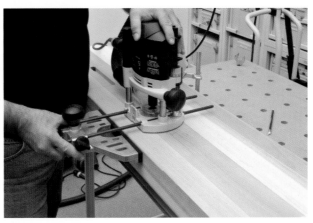

When the edge guide is properly set, align the router for the start of the cut, plunge…

After roughly setting the router, it can be micro-adjusted to the center line. Loosen the large knob on the guide and use the green adjustment knob to align the OF 1400 with the center mark.

…and make the groove.

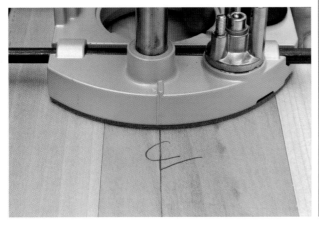

Double check the alignment and lock with the guide knob.

The result.

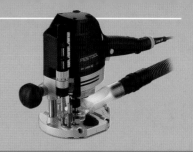

Using the OF 1040 & OF 1400 with the Festool Guide Rail System

To use the OF 1040 and OF 1400 with the Festool Guide Rail system requires two accessories, a two-piece guide stop and a support.

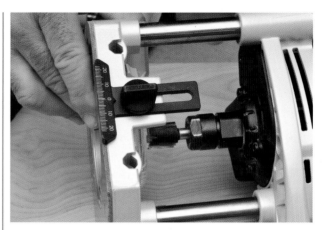

The support installs on the side of the router.

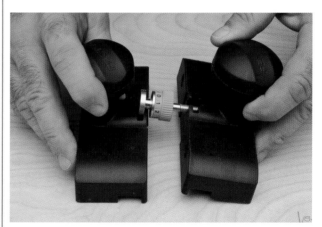

The micro-adjuster on one of the guide stop units connects to the other by placing the disc in the slot.

Run the two rods through the holes and tighten with the knobs.

The guide stops can be adjusted to the guide rail with the screw underneath. They should run smoothly, but evenly on the guide rail.

For fine tuning the alignment, next loosen the large knob on the inner part of the guide stop....

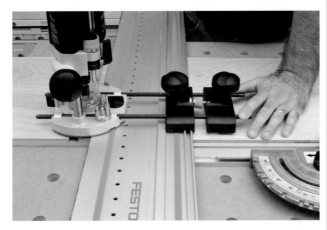

This is the standard set up for the guide stop with the groove of the inner piece running on the out channel of the guide rail. Holding the router in position, set the support so it touches the work surface.

...and use the micro-adjuster to finalize the alignment with center. Retighten. It is important that the knob on the outer part of the guide stop remain tightened during this adjustment.

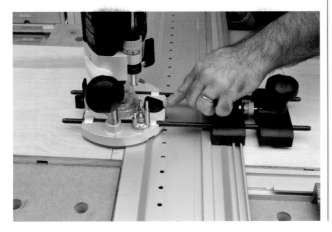

For rough adjustment, loosen the knob on the router base and align to the center line. Retighten the knob.

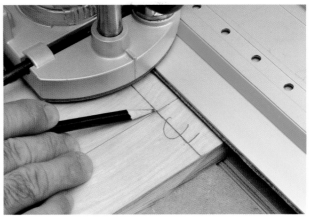

In this example, the object is to create a stop dado cut at this point.

To do this, the support scale is used. Already set to stabilize and level the router on the rail, it can now be used to calculate the end of the cut when using metric bits. The bit is 18mm, which means 9mm on either side of center. Therefore the router is moved on the rail so the scale is aligned on the stop line at 9mm…

…pushing it along the guide rail…

…and the limit stop is placed on the rail to hold the position.

…until you reach the limit stop.

After setting the cut, plunge the router…

The result.

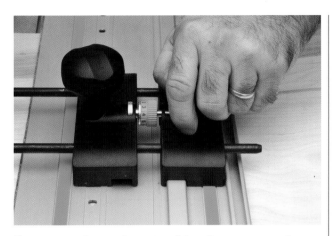

If you ever need to use the router off the rail, you can move the guide stop to this second position, with the outer part riding on this extrusion.

The adjustments are similar to the other rail position, except that for micro-adjustments the knob on the outer part is loosened and the other remains tight.

Off-rail operations require a hard fiber base runner, which raises the router to the level of the guide. It simply clips into place. It has a 20mm hole, but it can be expanded up to 36mm by plunging with a bit.

Note: A common error is to try to make the guide stop run on both extrusions. It is not intended to be used in this way and cancels out the micro-adjustment capability.

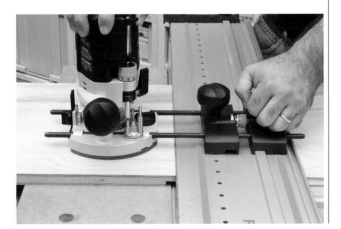

With the hard fiber base runner in place, the router runs level on the rail. The support is no longer needed for support, but its scale is still useful.

OF 2200 EB

At 2200 watts, the OF 2200 is the most powerful router in the Festool line. This gives it the strength to easily plunge into the hardest maple or make a 1/2" groove with a single pass. At the same time, the ergonomic design makes it easy to maneuver and control. Despite its strength, it is still portable and is perfect for the job site or the shop. It is loaded with features that make it faster, easier, and smarter.

Includes

Chip catcher	●
Collet—1/2"	●
Dust extraction hood	●
Standard U.S. guide bushing adapter	●
Systainer	SYS 4

Specifications

Collet diameter range	1/4", 1/2", and 8 mm
Drive shaft speed	10,000 - 22,000 rpm
Power consumption	2200 watts / 18 amps
	120 v AC
Quick depth adjustment range	3 5/32"
Weight	17.2 lbs.

PERFORMANCE

• **2200 Watt Motor.** The sheer strength of the OF 2200 makes it one of the most powerful routers available!

• **1/2" Collet.** The 1/2" collet of the OF 2200 takes full advantage of its 2200 Watts of power.

• **Large Bit Capacity.** The standard base for the OF 2200 router has a 3-3/8" opening, enough room for the largest of router bits.

• **MMC Electronics.** Equipped with electronic controls, Festool routers maintain constant speed under load, improving cut quality. Multi-Material Control (MMC) electronics also allows for step-less variable speed for different applications, and overload protection for longer life.

• **Magnetic Spindle Brake.** The Magnetic Spindle Brake offers a fast, reliable method of retarding spindle motion, while prolonging the service life of the motor.

PRECISION

• **80mm Plunge Depth Capacity.** The deep, 3-1/4" plunge depth gives great versatility to the OF 2200. The collet plunges 10mm below the base of the router for added ease in changing bits.

• **Precision Depth Adjustment.** Micro-adjustability to 1/256" (0.1 mm) allows tremendous precision while routing. Indents at each 0.1 mm increment.

• **Double Locking Plunge Columns.** The locking mechanism engages both of the anodized plunge columns to prevent movement. The plunge depth is locked with a single twist of the locking knob located on the router's handle.

• **Four Position Depth Stop Turret.** The four position depth stop turret provides four pre-configurable plunge depths, plus a 5/64" (2mm) finishing pass setting.

• **Locking Depth Stop Rod.** Save time by locking the OF 2200 in its plunged position and calibrate the plunge depth using the four-position depth stop turret in a single step.

• **Triple Bearing Design.** Bearings at the top, middle and bottom make the spindle less likely to wobble and reduce bit deflection. This is particularly important considering the sheer power of the OF 2200 and the centrifugal forces exerted with spinning large bits at speeds up to 22,000 RPM.

EASE OF USE

• **30° Handle Offset.** The 30° offset creates a comfortable and natural working position. In this handle configuration the application of forward motion to the router also applies lateral force against the edge of the work piece. When using the Edge Guide, this force keeps the guide against the material.

• **Control Placement.** The OF 2200 power trigger, trigger lock, locking knob for the double-column plunge depth lock and release trigger for the 360° dust shroud are intuitively placed for ease of use. Controls are clearly labeled with icons indicating purpose and adjustment direction.

• **Quad Center Line Marks.** The OF 2200 has a center line indention on each side of the base, providing a visual reference point for aligning the center of the bit with the cut line.

• **Supportive Base.** The sub-base is designed to prevent scratches, to glide easily, and offer a large, flat surface.

• **Tool-Less Hinged Base System.** Changing or attaching bases is fast and simple. Insert the two base hinges into their slots and snap the base securely in place in seconds. This base system makes it easy to access template guides which are secured under the base.

• **Self-Centering Template Guide Socket.** Template guides click into a self-centering, magnetic, keyed socket and are held securely under the router base after it is replaced.

• **Single-Tool Ratcheting Collet.** The spindle locking lever disengages spindle movement and loosens the collet with a ratcheting motion. The ingenious retractable 360° dust shroud and wide plunge column spacing enables open access to the collet.

WORK FLOW

• **Dust Extraction Column.** The Dust Extraction Column is at the back of the OF 2200 and extends to the top of the router and includes a swivel nozzle, keeping the power cord (also top mounted) and dust extraction hose out of your way. Festool recommends using a 36mm hose.

• **Retractable, Spring-Loaded 360° Dust Shroud.** The shroud maximizes dust extraction while providing high visibility of the work piece. The shroud retracts back into the locked position after the router is fully plunged. It is released with an easily accessible lever.

ACCESSORIES

• **Base Accessory Kit.** The OF 2200 Base Accessory Kit offers a variety of application specific bases to aid with dust extraction when using smaller router bits.

• **Guide Rail Adapter.** The Guide Rail Adapter included in the OF 2200 Base Accessory Kit, sold separately, enables attachment of the OF 2200 to the Festool Guide Rail System. With a fine micro-adjuster knob, it adjusts in increments of 1/256" (0.1 mm). It can be attached or removed with a twist of the single locking knob.

• **Edge Guide System.** With a fine micro-adjustment of 1/256" (0.1 mm), the Edge Guide offers unparalleled precision. It attaches to the OF 2200 with two rods and a single locking knob, allowing fast attachment and removal.

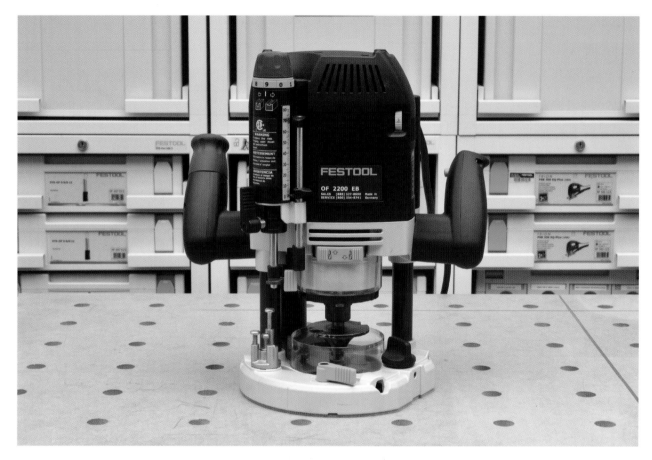

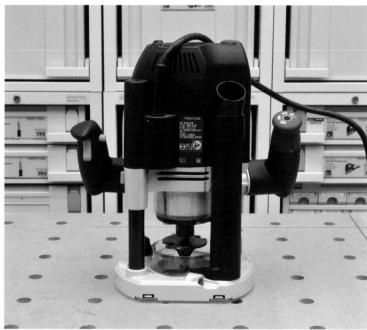

Overview of the OF 2200

Like the OF 1400, the OF 2200 has a ratchet system for bit removal. This is the switch.

The trigger and trigger lock are conveniently located on one handle.

The OF 2200 has a 360° dust shroud that is spring-loaded. The green switch at the left in this photo releases the shroud into position.

The plunge depth lock is on the other handle, where it can be engaged with a twist of the wrist.

When the router is fully plunged, it retracts back into the locked position.

Lock indicator.

The exhaust port is at the back of the router.

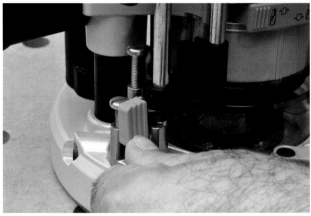

When the depth rod is roughly set, the green lever locks it in place during fine tuning.

The base plate snaps into place. The green lever releases and locks the plate.

The final depth can be set precisely by following a few simple steps.
1. Plunge the router down to the material, aligning the profile to the edge.

The turret has four positions plus a 5/64" (2mm) finishing pass setting on the shortest turret.

2. Use the left handle to lock in place.

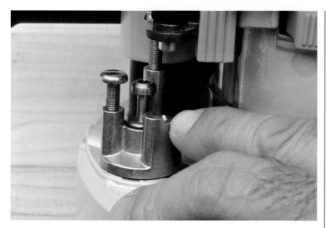

3. Turn the turret to the final depth stop setting, the lower step of the shortest turret, with a point sticking out of the middle. The upper step will is used for the next to the last cut, setting up a smooth 5/64" final pass.

4. Loosen the depth rod clamping lever.

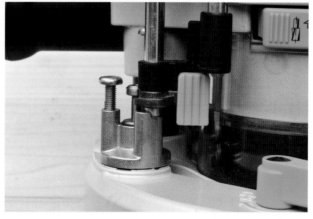

5b. Lower the rod so it engages the bottom stop of the turret.

6. Engage the green lever of the eccentric depth rod lock.

7. Tighten the depth rod locking lever.

10. Relock the column lock at the handle.

8. Release the column lock.

11. Release the eccentric lock, and it's ready to go.

9. Now, with a straight edge or piece of wood, use the micro-adjuster to maximize the profile.

With an aggressive cut the turret allows you to make 4 passes. Two of the turrets can be adjusted to determine how much material is removed in the rough cuts.

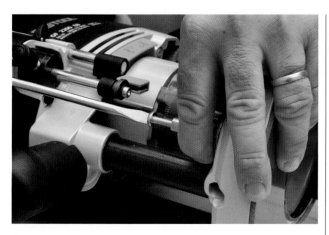

Simply turn the turret screw to the desired level and check against the edge to be routed.

Make the run.

The turrets give four levels of depth, but it is not always necessary to use all the passes. In this example, the bit used here does not cut at the shallowest level, so we can move to the second level. Turn the turret so the screw is under the depth rod.

The result.

The shortest post on the turret has no adjustment screw, but is stepped. The raised portion is 2mm above the final position, meaning that the last cut will be a finish cut, removing little material. Turn the turret so the rod comes to rest on the raised step.

Make the run.

Run.

The result.

The last shallow pass (2mm) gives a particularly smooth final cut.

Turn the turret slightly so the rod rests on the lower step.

For reinstallation, the two tabs on the base accessories fit into slots in the housing, and the base pivots up and locks.

Accessories & Attachments for the OF 2200 EB

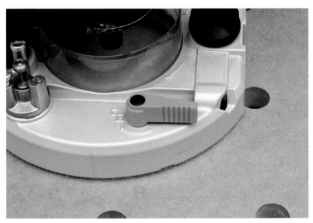

The green locking lever on the top of the base allows for rapid removal of accessories to the base.

Inserts are installed with the base removed. They align with four indexing pins…

Turn to the unlocked position and pivot the base off.

…and are held in place with two earth magnets.

With the insert in place, reinsert the bottom plate.

An accessory plate is available for template guides that fully support the guide, reducing the chance of tipping when used with a template. The plate snaps into place.

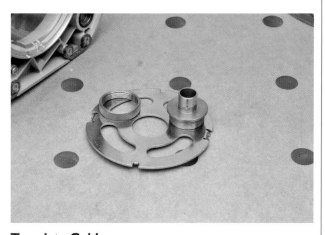

Template Guides

The universal template guide automatically centers.

Festool manufacturers a range of template guides to fit various bits. They are available in either metric or imperial sizes.

It pops into place.

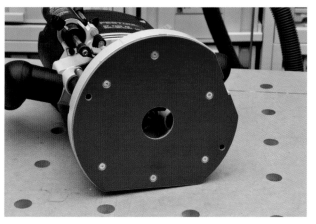

A small bore base is also available as an accessory, designed to provide more stability when using smaller profile bits.

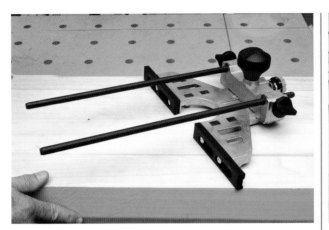

The Edge Guide

The edge guide and rods work much as they do on the OF 1400.

Tighten the rods in the guide and slide into the router base. Loosen the large knob on the edge guide, align the center of the bit with the center of the groove, and snug the edge guide against the material.

Fine tune the alignment with the micro-adjuster, then tighten the knob.

Run the router. Notice that the router is designed with an ergonomic angle of 30 degrees. This allows effortless two-handed operation, giving great control and support to the router during operation. This will be a deep groove so I will make it in two passes, using the turret for a shallower pass first.

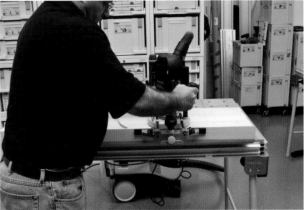

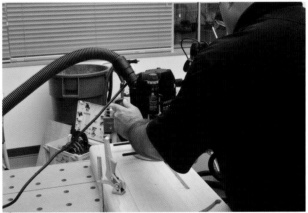

Another view.

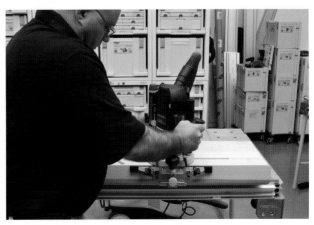

Turn the turret to finished setting and cut again.

The result.

Table Widener

A table widener is also available for the OF 2200.

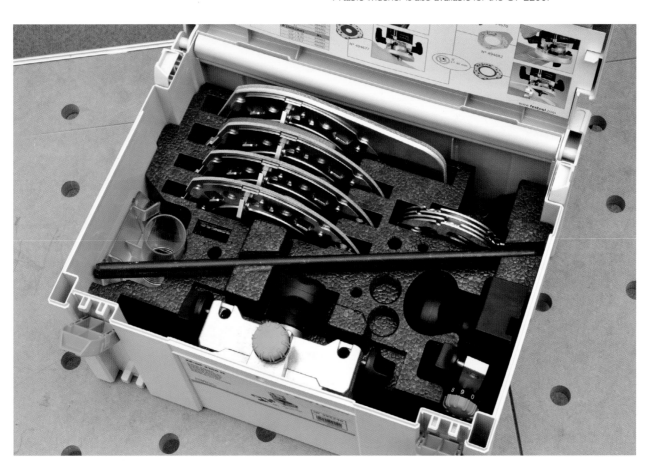

Accessory Kit for the OF 2200

The accessory kit includes the parallel edge guide, the guide stop, guide rods, a table widener, the small bore base, the template guide base, the offset base for the guide rail, and template guides. The kit comes with either metric or imperial guides.

The guide stop rides on the outer extrusion, with the rods running through the router base and locked in position.

Using the OF 2200 with the Festool Guide Rail System

The guide stop integrates the OF 2200 with the Festool guide rail system.

For micro-adjustment, loosen the large knob on the guide stop…

An accessory base adapts the router for use with the guide rail system. It has a 5mm offset ledge that supports the router when it is on the guide rail. There is a place for the support, which is useful for the stop dado, but, as this is a more substantial router, the base plate provides much better support.

…and dial the adjustment.

To set the depth, release the column lock...

...and plunge the router down so the bit touches the material.

Reengage the column lock

Turn the turret so the lowest tower is beneath the depth rod.

Set the micro-adjuster to zero.

Release the depth rod locking lever.

Lock the depth rod with the lever.

Bring the depth rod down so it touches the turret.

Release the column lock.

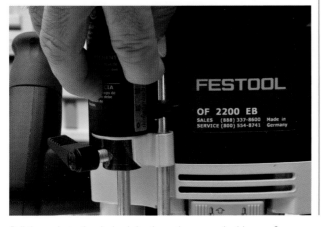

Pull the scale to the desired depth on the gauge, in this case 8mm.

Now it can be micro-adjusted. The graphics are helpful in remembering which direction to turn the adjuster. Turn the adjuster clockwise for a deeper cut,

...and counterclockwise for a shallower cut.

Guides & Jigs for the OF 1010, OF 1400, & OF 2200

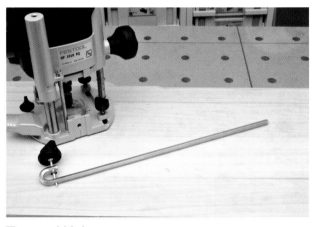

Trammel Unit

The trammel unit allows for routing circles and curved trim up to 29-7/8" diameter. The pivot is pointed and 4mm in diameter. Designed for the OF 1040, it can also be used with the OF 1400 by filling the empty rod slot.

The button on the back of the right handle releases the dust shroud.

The shroud simply lifts out of the way.

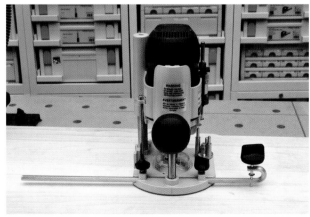

The trammel fits through the front slot and is tightened with the two knobs.

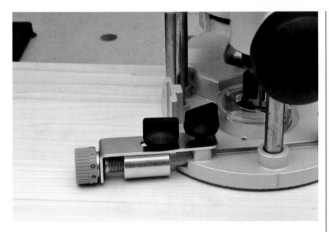

The micro-adjuster can be added for fine adjustments.

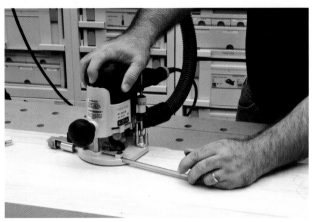

Set the router for the desired depth and make the cut.

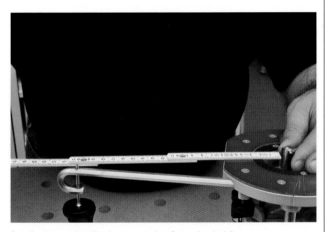

Set the internal radius by measuring from the inside flute of the bit to the point.

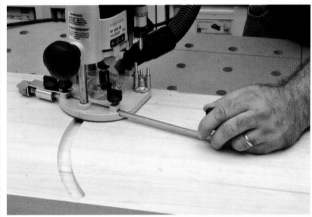

The result.

Drill a 4mm hole at the pivot/center of the arc.

Guides & Jigs for the OF 1010, OF 1400, & OF 2200

The Plexiglas Edge Slot Template for the OF 1010, OF 1400, & OF 2200

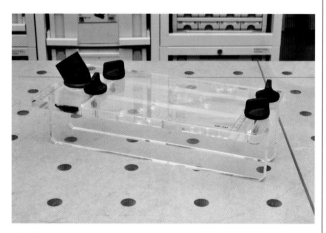

The Plexiglas template is used for routing grooves and slots on edges. It is designed to work with all three portable routers.

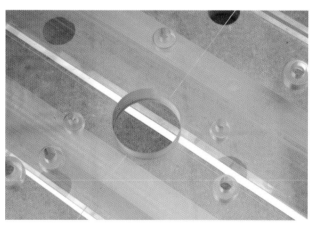

Etched center lines aid in alignment.

Scribe a line that will be the center of the cut.

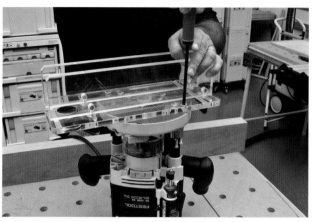

Attach the template to the base plate using two screws.

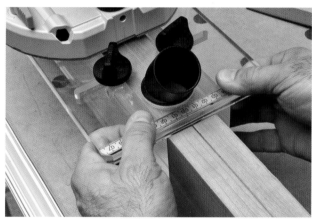

Align the template on the center lines, using the scale at the end. Move the walls of the jig snug to the work piece and tighten.

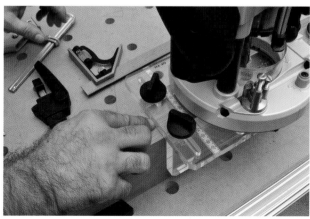

Do the same at the other end.

On a long slot with this jig, two extraction lines can be used.
Insert a Y adapter in the CT unit.

Reset the turret to the final setting and make a second run.

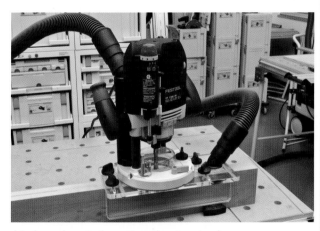

Attach one hose to the router exhaust port and one
to the port on the template.

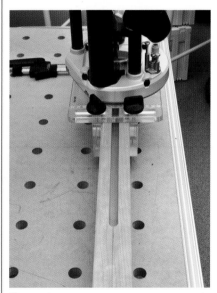

The result.

Set the depth for the final cut, then use the turret
to make the first run shallower.

A hint. Clamps can be used to create positive limit stops.

The MFS 400 & MFS 700 Multi-Routing Template

These versatile guides can be used with all three Festool portable routers to make the routing of circles, and precise inside and outside cuts easy and efficient. The anodized aluminum frame with integrated rule can be adjusted to an accuracy of 1/32". By combining sets, the sizes they can accommodate are unlimited. They are designed for use with the Festool Guide Rail System.

The profiles of the MFS 400 are 7-7/8" x 3-1/8" and 15-3/4" x 3-1/8". The maximum interior dimensions are 4-11/16" x 12-9/16". The maximum circle diameter is 34".

The MFS 700 is 15-3/4" x 3-1/8" and 27-1/2" x 3-1/8". The maximum interior dimensions are 12-9/16" x 24-7/16". The maximum circle diameter is 51".

The MFS kits come with clamping flanges, tilt protector, circle routing insert, pivot point, and adjustment tool.

A routing slide is available as an accessory. It enables the router to ride on carriage for routing cut-outs over large areas.

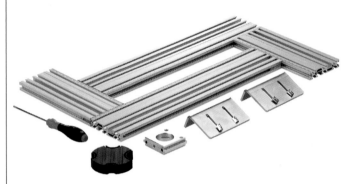

MFS 400 Multi-Routing Template

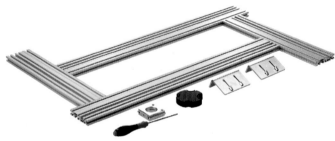

MFS 700 Multi-Routing Template

Routing slide

VS 600 Jointing System

All three Festool portable routers can be used in the VS 600 jointing system. It makes the laborious task of dovetail joints fast and easy. Simply clamp the template in the jig, place the work piece against the swivel stop, secure the work piece, fine adjust with the eccentric memory ring and rout. Seven different joint types are available with working lengths up to 24". The template swings out of the way so results can be checked at any time.

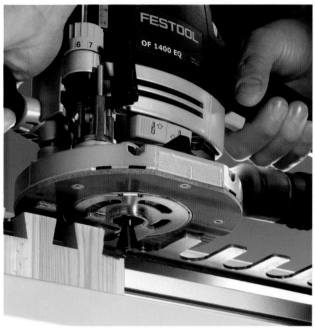

Hole Drilling Set

Guide plate, centering mandrel, linear stops, and two edge stops for drilling European 32 mm grid pattern holes in shelves and cabinets.

2. THE MFK 700 TRIM ROUTER

2. THE MFK 700 TRIM ROUTER

The modular design of the MFK 700 means it can be easily transformed from a horizontal to a vertical position without tools in a few simple steps. Light and maneuverable, the MFK 700 can be used to trim laminate and edge band or to rout grooves for inlays. 1/256" (0.1 mm) fine depth adjustments and exceptional dust extraction make this an ideal router for a variety of light routing tasks.

Includes

1.5° Horizontal base and feeler bearing set	Included with set option
Collets	1/4" & 8 mm
Dust extraction hood	●
Plug-it power cord	●
Standard threaded base for U.S. guide bushing	●
Systainer	SYS 2 included with set option
Vertical base	●

Specifications

Column stroke	9/16"
Drive shaft speed	10,000 - 26,000 RPM
Maximum bit diameter	1"
Power consumption	720 watts / 6.0 amps
Weight	4.2 lbs

PERFORMANCE

• **MMC Electronics.** Equipped with electronic controls, Festool routers maintain constant speed under load, improving cut quality. MMC electronics also allow for step-less variable speed for different applications, and overload protection for longer life.

• **720 Watt Motor.** The 720 Watt motor provides enough power for most trimming, profiling, and routing applications. It utilizes onboard thermal monitoring to protect against overload and soft start technology ensures long service life.

PRECISION

• **Super Fine Micro-Adjustment.** The MFK 700's super fine micro-adjuster knob fine tunes the cut depth to an accuracy of 0.1 mm. The micro-adjuster knob is clearly labeled to show which direction the bit will move. When the depth is correctly set, dual locking knobs prevent movement.

• **Control.** The vertical and horizontal bases have integrated guide handles that provide comfort and control while routing. They are also one of two mechanisms for locking the micro-adjustable depth of cut.

EASE OF USE

• **Quad Center Line Marks.** The MFK 700 has a center line indention on each side of the base, providing a visual reference point for aligning the center of the bit with the cut line.

• **Tool-Less Base System.** The MFK comes with both horizontal and vertical bases that can be easily changed without tools. Three turns of the locking knob loosens or tightens the locking mechanism.

• **Wide Bases.** Both bases offer a large, stable bearing surface, giving better control of the router. The base plate material is designed to prevent scratches, glide easily, and create a stable & flat bearing surface.

• **Template Guides.** The vertical base includes a threaded insert which accepts template guides adding to the overwhelming versatility of this router.

• **One Wrench Collet.** A push of a button locks the spindle so the collet can be loosened or tightened with a single wrench. A 1/4" collet is standard, but an 8 mm collet is available.

WORK FLOW

• **Dust Extraction.** Like all Festool power tools, the MFK 700 is integrated with the dust extraction system, including a variety of dust extraction options for every possible application. The dust and debris are removed from around the bit so visibility is increased and clean-up time is nearly eliminated.

• **Swivel Dust Extraction Connector.** The swivel connector allows the dust extractor hose to move freely and prevents binding.

• **Parallel Edge Guide.** The Parallel Edge Guide is used to create straight, accurate trenches and grooves and with edge routing. The Parallel Edge Guide features a super fine micro-adjustment which allows fine tuning in increments of 0.1 mm! It comes with a dust extraction shroud to ensure effective particle removal.

The MFK 700 comes as a kit that includes the motor unit, the vertical and 1.5° horizontal bases and bearing set, dust shrouds, and power cords, all in a handy Systainer.

The MFK 700 Trim Router

There are two pins on the front of the MFK 700 motor to connect it to the bases. One is notched.

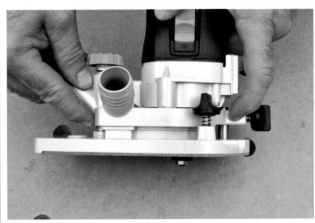

The router has two columns for stability.

The notched pin is inserted into the socket with the knob lock, which is used to secure it.

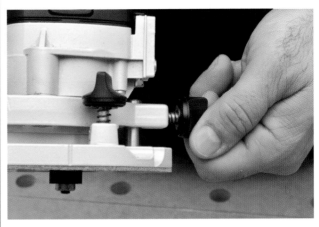

One column is locked with this small knob....

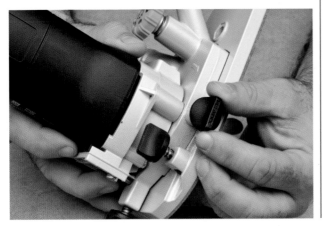

The motor is inserted into the base and locked in place.

...and the other by turning the handle knob.

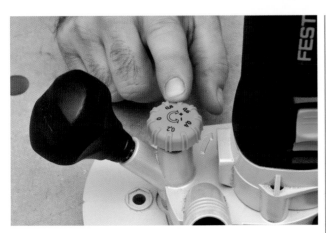

This is the adjustment knob used to make both large and micro-adjustments. It adjusts the motor assembly on the columns. Each notch in the dial represents a 0.1mm adjustment to the bit height. To use, first release both column locks.

...and the handle knob. When the rough depth is set, the adjust knob is used to make the necessary finer adjustments.

With the columns unlocked, turn the adjuster to bring the bit to the approximate position desired.

The plate is threaded...

Lock the small knob...

...to accommodate and center the template guide.

Bits are installed with the motor removed from the base. Depress the arbor lock and turn the arbor nut with a wrench to loosen or tighten.

The base of the MFK 700 has a socket into which a connecting rod will fit.

It is useful for controlling the router in tight situations like this.

Trimming Laminates

The laminate, no-file bit has a chamfer flute at the top…

…over a flush trim vertical flute. At the bottom is a nylon bearing.

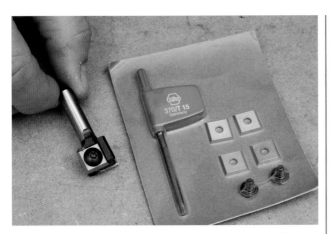

The HW Replacable Knife Bit has changeable blades, each with four edges. It may be turned as it dulls, and when all four edges are used the blade can be readily replaced.

With an overhang of over 3/4", the lower dust shroud needs to be removed, so it does not interfere with the cut, and the dust hose attached to the port on the top of the base.

When the overhang of the laminate is less than 3/4" you can use the dust shroud under the plate. It screws into a threaded socket. A directional dust port is added.

It is always wise to do a test before doing the finished work. Attach a piece of the laminate to a piece of straight-edged scrap.

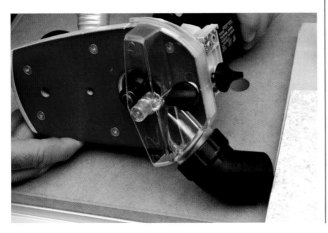

This shroud acts as a chip collector giving dust extraction from below.

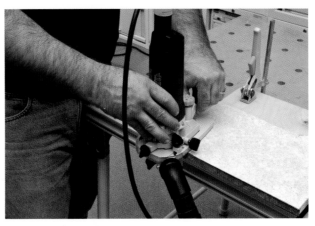

With the router set at the best approximation of depth run a test. Start by going straight in until the bearing meets the front edge.

The MFK 700 Trim Router

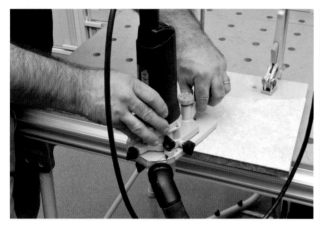

Turn the router until the back of the dust shroud hits the edge of the work piece. This insures that the chip is directed toward the port. Make the run.

...and the knob handle.

By running a fingernail up the front edge, you can feel if the cut is clean. If the chamfer is too bold or you can see the substrate underneath, you are set too deeply and need to make the cut shallower. I can still feel a slight overhang, meaning that the cut is too shallow and the router needs to be adjusted for a deeper cut.

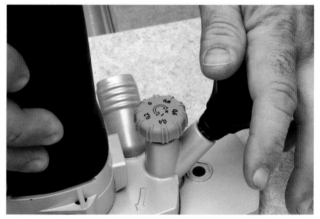

Turn the micro-adjuster to a deeper position. This should be a small adjustment, since we approximated the depth before starting. Turning 0.2 or 0.3 mm should be enough. Remember, each notch is 0.1 mm.

To adjust, loosen the small knob…

Recut the test laminate.

A great result.

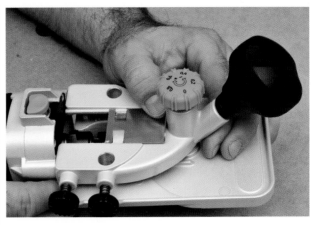

When using dust extraction with the horizontal base, open the slider.

Using the Horizontal Base for Edge Banding

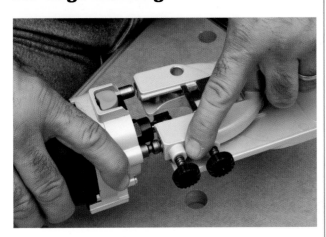

The 1.5° horizontal base is attached to the pins in the same way, with the notched pin going into the hole with the knob lock. The base gets its name because it trims the edge 1.5 degrees off of horizontal so it will not scratch the top surface.

The dust shroud fits over the slider, with the notched pin going into the hole and tightened in place with the knob.

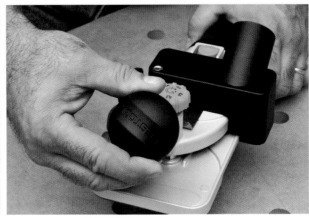

Before making adjustments, unlock the knob handle.

The MFK 700 Trim Router

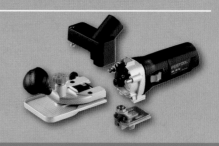

All adjustments are made with the green micro-adjuster.

The sensor bearing attaches to the bottom. Remove the two screws.

Orient the bit so the flute is in its uppermost position and lay a block on the work surface. You will be able to see any gaps.

Lay the bearing unit in place and secure with the same screws.

Adjust until the block rests flat on the plate and the bit flute.

The sensor bearing is adjustable by releasing the green knob and sliding it to the desired depth.

The shaped base will let you get into corners edge banding up to 3 mm thick.

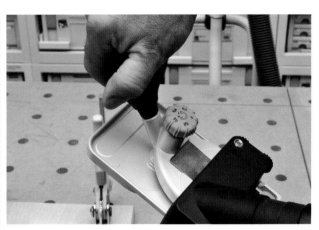

The micro-adjuster can be used to fix this too aggressive cut. Begin by loosening the knob.

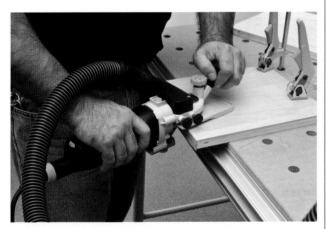

In the horizontal configuration, the router is operated with the left hand on the front knob, and a pulling motion toward the operator.

Turn the micro-adjuster in the minus direction (counterclockwise). I'll start with 0.4 mm...

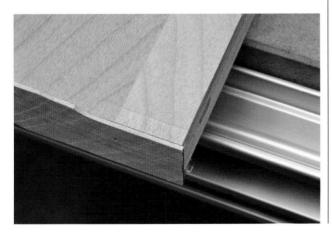

If the cut is too deep it goes into the top surface.

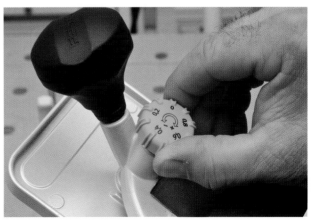

...and adjust as necessary ...

...until the cut is smooth.

Inlaid Edge Banding

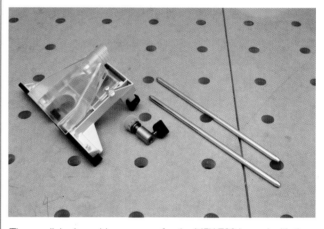

The parallel edge guide accessory for the MFK 700 is used with the vertical base to create the running channel for inlaid edge banding. It consists of the guide, a dust shroud, two connecting rods, and a micro-adjuster.

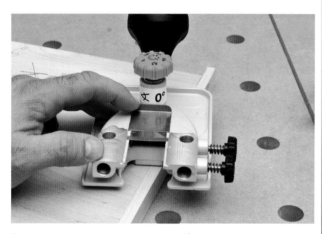

For thicker edge banding where the 1.5° chamfering may be overly noticeable, a zero degree horizontal base is available as an accessory.

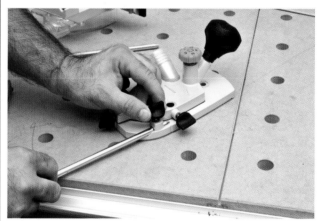

Install the rods into the slots on the vertical base and tighten.

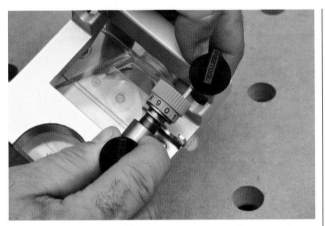

The micro-adjuster is used for fine changes to the alignment. Like the other Festool adjusters, each whole number represents 0.1 mm (1/256").

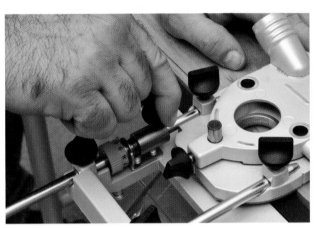

Tighten the lock nut on the micro-adjuster...

The micro-adjuster is placed on the connecting rod between the base plate and the parallel edge guide. The space between the green dial and the collar fits into a bracket on the guide. Alignment begins by loosening the lock knobs on the guide.

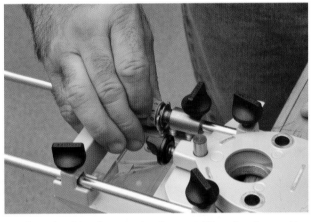

...and use the dial to fine tune the alignment. When the alignment is complete, lock the guide to the connector rods.

Having determined the center line of the banding and scribed it on the work piece, align the indicator on the base plate with the center line and pull the parallel edge guide snug against the work piece.

To adjust the depth of the channel, begin by releasing the depth locks here and on the other side.

The MFK 700 Trim Router

Lay the banding on the surface of the plate and adjust the blade so it is slightly below the surface of the banding.

Make the first cut.

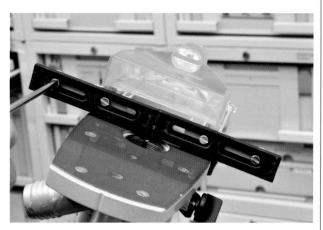

For the banding operation, the fence of the edge guide can be adjusted so the two halves meet...

As expected, the banding is a little proud.

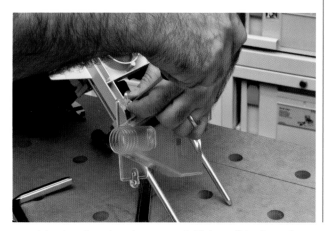

...and the dust shroud can be removed. All dust will be drawn from the top and the shroud is not needed.

Turn the micro-adjuster clockwise for a deeper cut.

Engage the depth locks.

Clean up the edges.

Recut the channel...

The result. With the router properly set, the channel placement is easily transferred to all pieces of the apron.

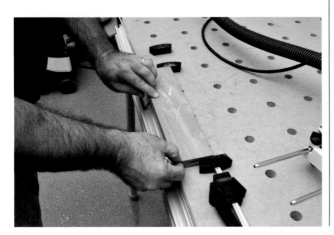

...and fit the banding.

3. Router Bits

Festool router bits are made from the finest materials available to the industry, binding tungsten-carbide powder with a cobalt binding material under extreme heat and pressure. This produces a dense material that is strong and wear resistant, leading to a long life of service. The bits are tested under the most rigorous conditions and applications to assure their ability to meet the craftsperson's needs.

HW Duro-Form Bits, 1/2" Shank

HW Duro-Form groove and edge-trimming bits with reversible carbide bits are ideal when you need long service life, high economy, and consistent precision. Key differences between carbide tipped Duro-Form and conventional carbide-tipped bits include

• Resharpening the blunt blades of conventional bits not only costs time and money but also reduces the diameter of this bit. This is not a problem with Duro-Form bits.

• Fast replacement of bits means sharp tools are readily available at all times.

• Guaranteed constant bit diameter, thanks to replaceable bits.

• Lower costs after purchase. One reversible bit lasts as long as two to four conventional bits and is thus extremely economical.

• The very hard-wearing reversible bits are exceptionally efficient, which means less cutting pressure is required and work is easier.

		700	1010	1400	2200	Item
1	Straight bit HW 8x20mm	–	–	●	●	491078
	Straight bit HW 10x25mm	–	–	●	●	491079
	Straight bit HW 12x30mm	–	–	●	●	491080

		700	1010	1400	2200	Item

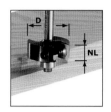

2   Rebating cutter HW 38mm   – – ● ●   491085

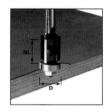

3   Flush trim bit HW 19/20mm   – – ● ●   491082

4   Edge trimming bit HW 30.5mm   – ● ● ●   491084

1/2" Shank Solid Surface Bits

Routing solid surface material is very demanding. It is tough work for people, machines, and especially the cutting tools. The right router bits take the tough out of routing solid surface material. Whether you are creating an edge profile, preparing a seam, or mounting a bowl, Festool router bits are designed to perform. Better cuts are a result of high quality carbide, keen bit construction, protective bearings, and well balanced design. Improve your results in less time with less work with Festool router bits.

		700	1010	1400	2200	Item

1   Solid TC spiral groove bit HW   – – ● ●   492660

		700	1010	1400	2200	Item
2	Edge trimming bit w/b HW 28mm	–	–	●	●	492706
3	Edge trimming bit w/b HW 19mm		–	●	●	492662
4	Basin bit w/bearing HW 53mm 18	–	–	●	●	492672
	Basin bit w/bearing HW 49mm 12	–	–	●	●	492673
	Basin bit w/bearing HW 45mm 6	–	–	●	●	492674
	Basin bit w/bearing HW 63mm 18	–	–	●	●	492678
	Basin bit w/bearing HW 59mm 12	–	–	●	●	492679
	Basin bit w/bearing HW 56mm 6	–	–	●	●	492680
5	Chamfer bit w/cutting edge HW 23mm	–	–	●	●	492664
6	Chamfer bit w/bearing, top HW 28mm	–	–	●	●	492704
7	Chamfer bit w/bearing HW 33.5mm	–	–	●	●	492666

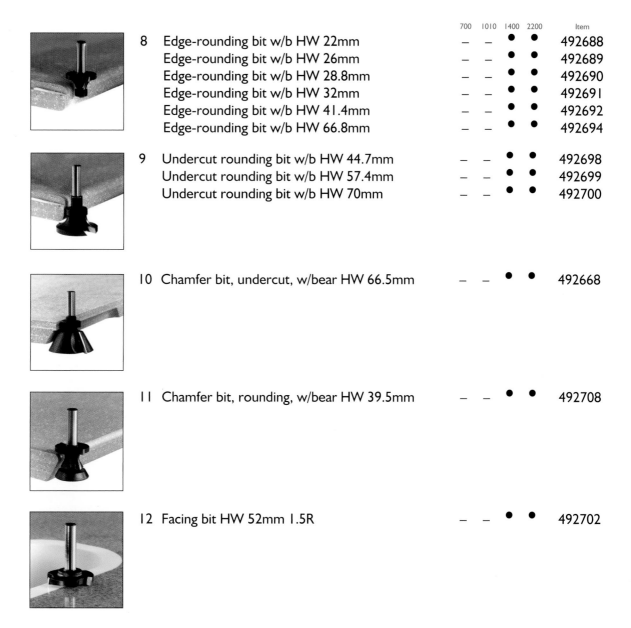

		700	1010	1400	2200	Item
8	Edge-rounding bit w/b HW 22mm	–	–	•	•	492688
	Edge-rounding bit w/b HW 26mm	–	–	•	•	492689
	Edge-rounding bit w/b HW 28.8mm	–	–	•	•	492690
	Edge-rounding bit w/b HW 32mm	–	–	•	•	492691
	Edge-rounding bit w/b HW 41.4mm	–	–	•	•	492692
	Edge-rounding bit w/b HW 66.8mm	–	–	•	•	492694
9	Undercut rounding bit w/b HW 44.7mm	–	–	•	•	492698
	Undercut rounding bit w/b HW 57.4mm	–	–	•	•	492699
	Undercut rounding bit w/b HW 70mm	–	–	•	•	492700
10	Chamfer bit, undercut, w/bear HW 66.5mm	–	–	•	•	492668
11	Chamfer bit, rounding, w/bear HW 39.5mm	–	–	•	•	492708
12	Facing bit HW 52mm 1.5R	–	–	•	•	492702

8mm Diameter Shank Bits

Festool carries a complete line of router bits in an 8 mm shank size. These provide 58% more volume than a 1/4" shank router bit. The greater the diameter reduces vibration and is more resistant to bending or breaking. Plus the larger shank allows you to use a larger diameter bit with your router.

		700	1010	1400	2200	Item
1	Roundover bit HW 42mm R6	–	•	•	•	491131

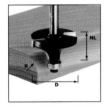

		700	1010	1400	2200	Item
2	Roundover bit w/ 2b HW 16.7mm	•	•	•	•	491009
	Roundover bit w/ 2b HW 18.7mm	•	•	•	•	491010
	Roundover bit w/ 2b HW 20.7mm	–	•	•	•	491011
	Roundover bit w/ 2b HW 22.7mm	–	•	•	•	491012
	Roundover bit w/ 2b HW 25.5mm	–	•	•	•	491013
	Roundover bit w/ 2b HW 28.7mm	–	•	•	•	491014
	Roundover bit w/ 2b HW 31.7mm	–	•	•	•	491015
	Roundover bit w/ 2b HW 38.1mm	–	•	•	•	491016
	Roundover bit w/ 2b HW 47.2mm	–	•	•	•	491017

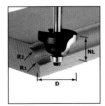

		700	1010	1400	2200	Item
3	Roman ogee bit w/b HW 31.7mm	–	•	•	•	491029
	Roman ogee bit w/b HW 38.1mm	–	•	•	•	491030

	700	1010	1400	2200	Item
4 Classical ogee bit HW 36.7mm	–	●	●	●	491031
5 Chamfer bit w/bear HW 24mm 30	–	●	●	●	491024
Chamfer bit w/bear HW 24mm 45	–	●	●	●	491025
Chamfer bit w/b HW 25.7mm 15	–	●	●	●	491132
Chamfer bit w/b HW 38.5mm 30	–	●	●	●	491133
6 Cove bit w/ b. guide HW 25.5mm	–	●	●	●	491018
Cove bit w/ b. guide HW 28.7mm	–	●	●	●	491019
Cove bit w/ b. guide HW 31.7mm	–	●	●	●	491020
Cove bit w/ b. guide HW 38.1mm	–	●	●	●	491021
7 Stile bit HW 43mm	–	●	●	●	491129
8 Reversible stile & rail bit 46mm	–	●	●	●	490645
9 Rail bit HW 43mm	–	●	●	●	491130

	700	1010	1400	2200	Item
10 Roundover bit w/angled bearing 17.5mm	–	●	●	●	491134
Roundover bit w/angled bearing 23.1mm	–	●	●	●	491135
Roundover bit w/angled bearing 31.4mm	–	●	●	●	491136
11 Bullnose bit HW 27mm	–	●	●	●	491139
12 Finger pull bit HW 22mm	–	●	●	●	491140
13 Hand hole bit HW 19mm	–	●	●	●	491033
14 Core box bit HW R4	–	●	●	●	490983
Core box bit HW R6.35	–	●	●	●	490984
Core box bit HW R8	–	●	●	●	490985
Core box bit HW R9.7	–	●	●	●	490986
Core box bit HW R12.7	–	●	●	●	490987
15 Raised pnl bit w/o b HW 42.7mm	–	●	●	●	491138

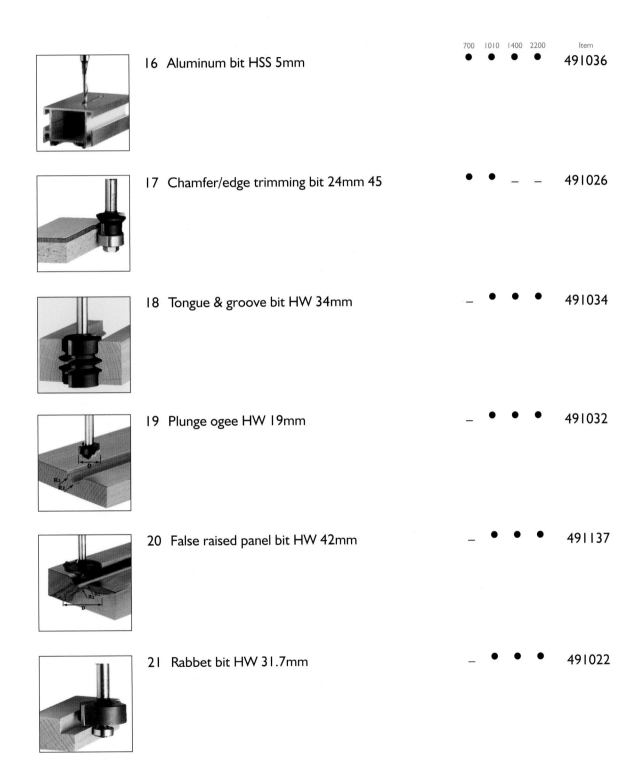

	700	1010	1400	2200	Item
16 Aluminum bit HSS 5mm	●	●	●	●	491036
17 Chamfer/edge trimming bit 24mm 45	●	●	–	–	491026
18 Tongue & groove bit HW 34mm	–	●	●	●	491034
19 Plunge ogee HW 19mm	–	●	●	●	491032
20 False raised panel bit HW 42mm	–	●	●	●	491137
21 Rabbet bit HW 31.7mm	–	●	●	●	491022

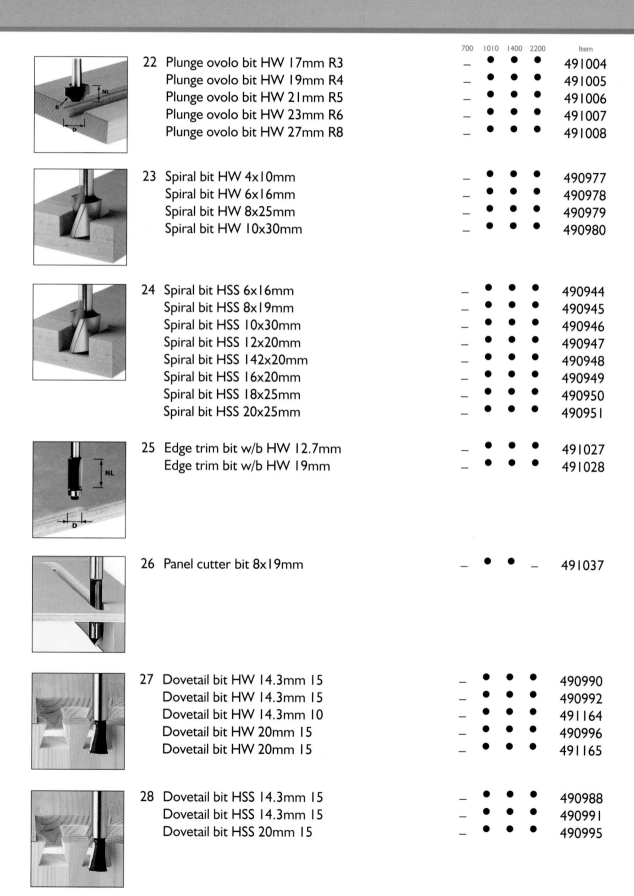

	700	1010	1400	2200	Item
22 Plunge ovolo bit HW 17mm R3	–	●	●	●	491004
Plunge ovolo bit HW 19mm R4	–	●	●	●	491005
Plunge ovolo bit HW 21mm R5	–	●	●	●	491006
Plunge ovolo bit HW 23mm R6	–	●	●	●	491007
Plunge ovolo bit HW 27mm R8	–	●	●	●	491008
23 Spiral bit HW 4x10mm	–	●	●	●	490977
Spiral bit HW 6x16mm	–	●	●	●	490978
Spiral bit HW 8x25mm	–	●	●	●	490979
Spiral bit HW 10x30mm	–	●	●	●	490980
24 Spiral bit HSS 6x16mm	–	●	●	●	490944
Spiral bit HSS 8x19mm	–	●	●	●	490945
Spiral bit HSS 10x30mm	–	●	●	●	490946
Spiral bit HSS 12x20mm	–	●	●	●	490947
Spiral bit HSS 142x20mm	–	●	●	●	490948
Spiral bit HSS 16x20mm	–	●	●	●	490949
Spiral bit HSS 18x25mm	–	●	●	●	490950
Spiral bit HSS 20x25mm	–	●	●	●	490951
25 Edge trim bit w/b HW 12.7mm	–	●	●	●	491027
Edge trim bit w/b HW 19mm	–	●	●	●	491028
26 Panel cutter bit 8x19mm	–	●	●	–	491037
27 Dovetail bit HW 14.3mm 15	–	●	●	●	490990
Dovetail bit HW 14.3mm 15	–	●	●	●	490992
Dovetail bit HW 14.3mm 10	–	●	●	●	491164
Dovetail bit HW 20mm 15	–	●	●	●	490996
Dovetail bit HW 20mm 15	–	●	●	●	491165
28 Dovetail bit HSS 14.3mm 15	–	●	●	●	490988
Dovetail bit HSS 14.3mm 15	–	●	●	●	490991
Dovetail bit HSS 20mm 15	–	●	●	●	490995

	700	1010	1400	2200	Item

29 Euro-hinge boring bit HW 20mm — • • • 491072
    Euro-hinge boring bit HW 35mm — • • • 491077

30 Dowel drill bit 3mm — • • — 491065
    Dowel drill bit 5mm — • • — 491064
    Dowel drill bit 5mm — • • — 491066
    Dowel drill bit 6mm — • • — 491067
    Dowel drill bit 8mm — • • — 491068
    Dowel drill bit 10mm — • • — 491069

31 Laminate slot cutter 40mm • • • — 491063

32 Straight/mortising bits
    Strait/mortise bit HW 3x6mm — • • • 490952
    Strait/mortise bit HW 4x10mm — • • • 490953
    Strait/mortise bit HW 5x12mm — • • • 490954
    Strait/mortise bit HW 6x14mm — • • • 490955
    Strait/mortise bit HW 7x17mm — • • • 490956
    Strait/mortise bit HW 8x20mm — • • • 490957
    Strait/mortise bit HW 9x23mm — • • • 490958
    Strait/mortise bit HW 10x20mm — • • • 490959
    Strait/mortise bit HW 10x25mm — • • • 490960
    Strait/mortise bit HW 11x20mm — • • • 490961
    Strait/mortise bit HW 12x20mm — • • • 490962
    Strait/mortise bit HW 13x20mm — • • • 490963
    Strait/mortise bit HW 14x20mm — • • • 490964
    Strait/mortise bit HW 15x20mm — • • • 490965
    Strait/mortise bit HW 16x20mm — • • • 490966
    Strait/mortise bit HW 16x30mm — • • • 490967
    Strait/mortise bit HW 18x20mm — • • • 490968
    Strait/mortise bit HW 18x30mm — • • • 490969
    Strait/mortise bit HW 19x20mm — • • • 490970
    Strait/mortise bit HW 20x20mm — • • • 490971
    Strait/mortise bit HW 20x30mm — • • • 490972
    Strait/mortise bit HW 22x20mm — • • • 490973
    Strait/mortise bit HW 24x20mm — • • • 490974
    Strait/mortise bit HW 25x20mm — • • • 490975
    Strait/mortise bit HW 30x20mm — • • • 490976

	700	1010	1400	2200	Item
33 HW Script bit 11mm	–	●	●	–	491002
34 HSS Script bit 11mm	–	●	●	–	491003
35 HSS Groove/slot bit 3mm	–	●	●	–	490941
HSS Groove/slot bit 4mm	–	●	●	–	490942
HSS Groove/slot bit 4mm	–	●	●	–	490943
36 Slot cutter HW 40x1.5mm	–	●	●	–	491038
Slot cutter HW 40x1.8mm	–	●	●	–	491039
Slot cutter HW 40x2mm	–	●	●	–	491040
Slot cutter HW 40x2.5mm	–	●	●	–	491056
Slot cutter HW 40x3mm	–	●	●	–	491057
Slot cutter HW 40x3.5mm		●	●	–	491058
Slot cutter HW 40x4mm	–	●	●	–	491059
Slot cutter HW 40x5mm	–	●	●	–	491060
37 Keyhole bit HW 10.5x13mm	–	●	●	●	491035
38 Two-edged V-groove bit HW 32x16mm 90	–	●	●	●	491001

Bits for use with MFK 700 EQ

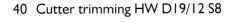

	700	1010	1400	2200	Item

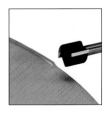

39 Cutter edge trimming HW D19/16   ● ● – – 491666

40 Cutter trimming HW D19/12 S8   ● ● – – 491670

41 Cutter edge trimming HW D19/16   ● ● – – 491667
Cutter edge trimming HW D19/16   ● ● – – 491668
Cutter chamfer HW D24/10 S8   ● ● – – 491669

42 Cutter trimming HW D19/12 S8   ● ● – – 491671
Cutter trimming HW D19/12 S8   ● ● – – 491672

43 Cutter trimming HW D19/12 S8   ● ● – – 491673
Cutter trimming HW D19/12 S8   ● ● – – 491674

44 Chamfer/edge trim bit HW 24mm   ● ● – – 491026

4. THE GUIDE RAIL SYSTEM

The TS plunge saws, and other Festool tools, work hand-in-hand with the guide rail system. Invented over 40 years ago, again and again the guide rail system has proven itself to be an essential element in accurate, efficient handling of these premium tools.

The rails come in eight sizes ranging from 32" (800 mm) to 197" (5000 mm). The rails join together to create almost limitless possibilities for nearly every work situation.

In addition there are rails in 42" (1080 mm) and 95" (2424 mm) that are used with the LR 32 hole-drilling system, making it easy to produce rows of holes for cabinets, casework, furniture, and shelf supports. The guide rails are used to precisely index the position of the router for creating the holes, and can also be used to created recessed for hardware like hinges.

The rails can be used in conjunction with the MFT tables or on their own. Soft, non-slip strips on the underside prevent damage to the work piece, and hold the guide rail securely in place.

The rails are equipped with a patented splinter guard, as described earlier. The splinter guard is cut by the blade on the first pass so it fits snuggly against the blade. Once cut, it represents the actual cut line of the saw so that it serves as a reference that can be pressed against the scribe line for an accurate cut. Due to this design a full scribe line is no longer needed. Simply mark the start and stop points, align the guide rail by the splinter guard to those points, and make the cut.

The saw and the guide rail work together, so the saw slides smoothly, producing a precise cutting tool that will remain constant over years of use.

Guide Rail features

• Zero clearance guide rail ensures that the cut mark matches the cut line.

• Quick set-up with non-slipping bottom strips

• Limit stops attached to the rail allow for repeat cuts.

• Effortless guidance of plunge saws or routers

• As part of an integrated system, it works with the Festool TS saws, OF routers, and PS jigsaws.

• Guide strips reduce surface friction with the saw base plate.

• Portable, lightweight, and precise.

• Connectors allow the creation of custom lengths.

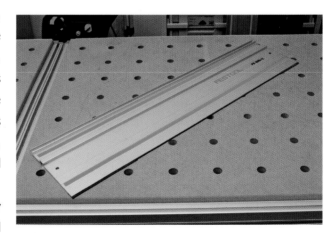

The heart of the system is the guide rail itself. Precision engineered of extruded aluminum, it comes in a 8 lengths ranging from 32 inches (800 mm) to 197 inches (5000 mm). Two others are available that are indexed to work with LR 32 hole drilling set for making shelf pin holes, Euro hinges and 32 mm hole space boring.

Model Name Item	FS 800/2 491 499	FS 1080/2 491 504	FS 1400/2 491 498	FS1900/2 491 503	FS2400/2 491 502	FS2700/2 491 937	FS3000/2 491 501	FS5000/2 491 500	FS1900/2-LR 32 491 6212	FS2424/2-LR 32 491 622
Length inches* Length mm*	32" 800mm	42" 1080mm	55" 1400mm	75" 1900mm	95" 2400mm	106" 2700mm	118" 3000mm	197" 5000mm	42" 1080mm	95" 2424mm

* Note: The metric dimensions are binding or absolute. Imperial measurements are coarse conversions.

Accessories

Model Name	Model No.
Angle unit, *for setting angles with the FS guide rails*	491 588
Deflector, *prevents suction hoses and cords from catching on the end of the guide rail.*	489 022
Limit stop, *provides front and rear stop position on guide rail*	485 827
Guide rail tote bag, *for up to two FS1400/2 or shorter guide rails.*	495 544
Gecko.	495 502
MFT Connector, *for connecting 2 MFT tables (two are needed) Note: MFT/3 does not connect to MFT 1080 or MFT 800.*	484 455
Table extension, useful when extra table length or width is needed	486 575
Stop flag, *for setting up multiple repeat cuts.*	495 542
Longitudinal stop, *adjustable.*	488 564

Clamps

FS-Rapid *clamp with fixed jaw, for clamping and positioning with Festool guide rails—includes fixed jaw and clamping jaw.*	489 790
Clamping profile, *for use with the FS-Rapid clamp to make a bar clamp. Length 32" (800mm)*	490 189
Quick clamp, *easily lock and quickly released for use with MFT and guide rails.*	491 594
Screw clamp, for securing guide rails.	
Clamping thickness 4 11/16" (120mm).	489 570
Clamping thickness 11 3/16" (300mm).	489 571
Clamping elements, for safe and exact fitting of workpiece	488 030

The guide rail assortment.

The Guide Rail System

The surface has two low friction glide strips.

This extrusion is the guide for TS saws and the OF routers. The channel below is for clamps and connectors.

This channel is used for clamping, connectors, and as a tool guide for the PS jigsaw and other tools.

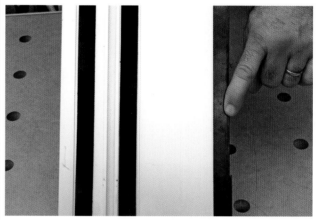

The replaceable splinter guard runs along one edge.

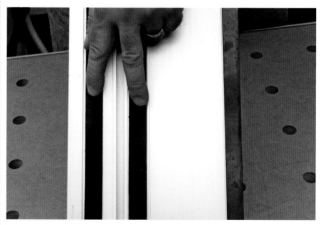

Two foam rubber strips hold the guide in place on the work surface, and are effective enough to obviate the need for clamping in many applications.

While it is always recommended that the guide rail be clamped in place, in some situations this is impossible. For quick and easy cuts, the rubber strips on the underside of the guide rail keep the guide rail from slipping. For critical and finish cut on expensive materials clamps should always be used.

As they wear, the friction glide strips, splinter guards and foam rubber gripper strips are easily replaced with self-adhesive strips.

Guide Rail Accessories

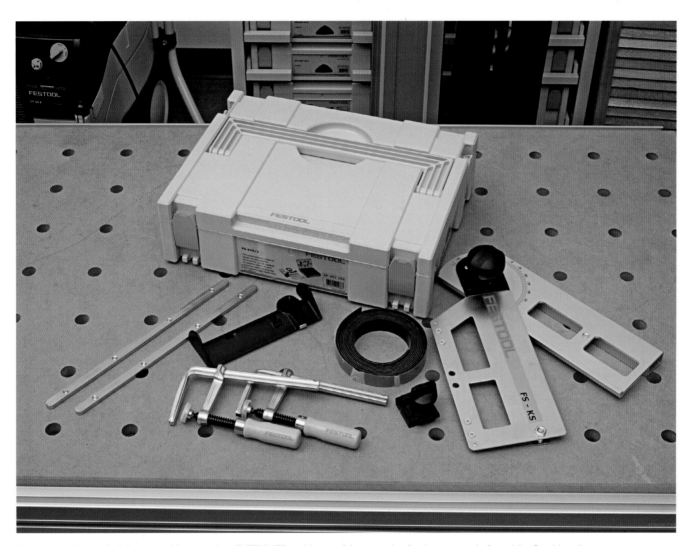

The optional Guide Rail Accessory Kit comes in a SYSTAINER and has useful accessories for the system. Left to right: 2 guide rail connectors, 2 clamps, a hose and power cord deflector, replacement splinter guard, 1 limit stop, and 1 angle unit.

CONNECTORS

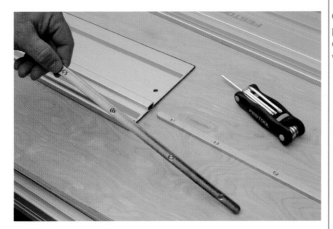

Guide rails are designed to be joined together to make longer pieces. This is done with connectors that fit into the channels. The connectors are fitted with slotted screws for fast and easy tensioning when joining rails.

To make the connection insert the connectors into one piece of guide rail, about half the length of the connector, and tighten. One connector tightens from the top, the other from the underside.

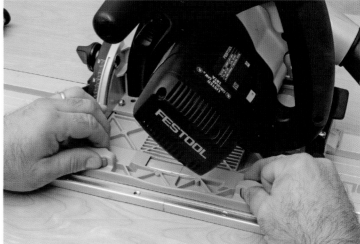

For fine tuning, a simple and accurate alignment can be made by bridging the joint with the saw on the guide rail and tightening the eccentric cam knobs.

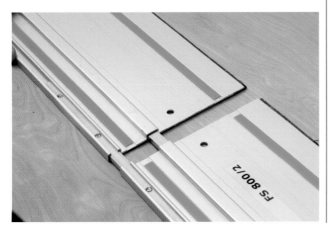

Insert the connectors into the other guide rail segment.

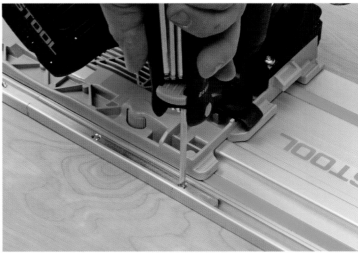

Tighten the exposed screws in the connector, then remove the saw, and tighten the screws beneath.

THE ANGLE UNIT

The FS-KS angle unit works with the guide rail to allow for accurate angle cutting.

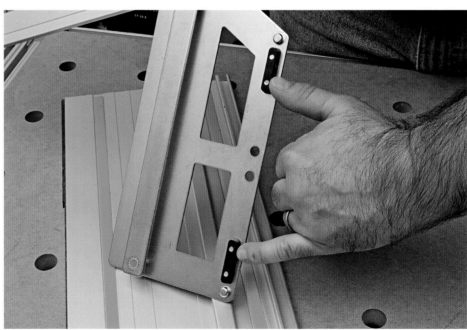

These keys in the bottom of the angle unit, run in the channel on the surface of the guide rail.

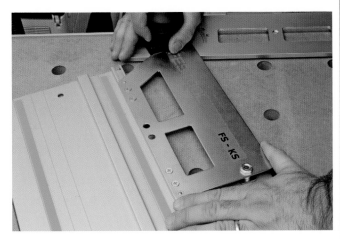

Place the angle unit in the channel and check for snugness. You want the unit to slide easily in the channel but with no play.

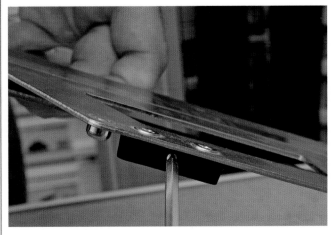

Each key has an adjustment screw.

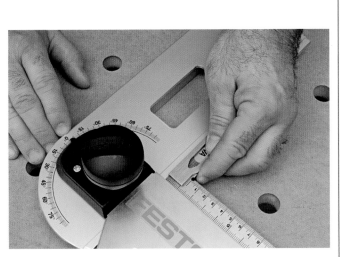

To check for true, set at 0° and hold a square in the angle.

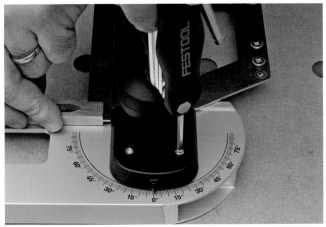

Loosen the two screws on top of the indicator and adjust as needed.

Guide Rail Accessories

The underside of the fence rides on the work piece.

To use, set the desired angle, place the angle unit in the guide rail, and position on the work piece.

Place the saw on the guide rail and make the cut.

LIMIT STOPS

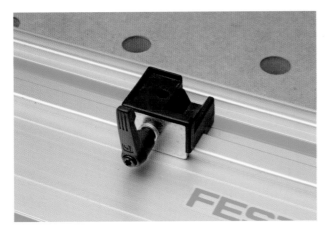 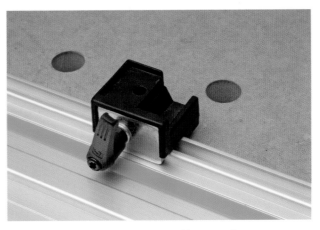

A limit stop can be attached to the guide rail to act as a positive stop for the tool. It can attach to either extrusion.

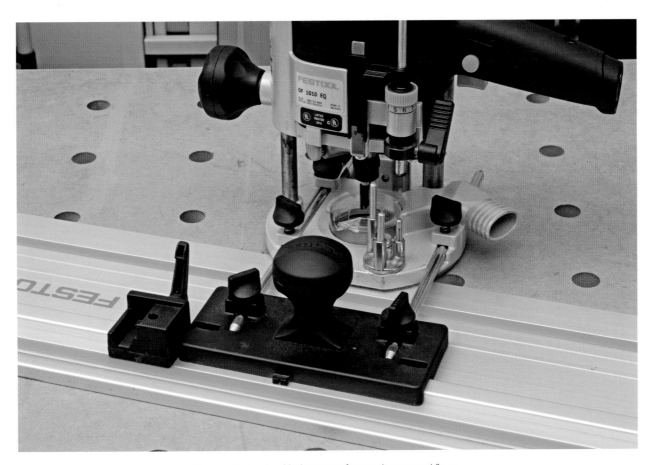

One application is with the router for creating stopped flutes.

THE GECKO

The Gecko is a lever-activated double suction cup material holder. Designed to work on non-porous surfaces, it has a number of uses, including carrying materials, and can lift or carry loads up to 110 lbs. With the guide rail attachment it is used to secure the guide rail to non-porous flat surfaces.

The underside has two large suction cups.

The Gecko with guide rail attachment rides in the outside channel of the guide rail.

Tighten the Gecko to the rail.

USING THE GUIDE RAIL WITH OTHER FESTOOL TOOLS

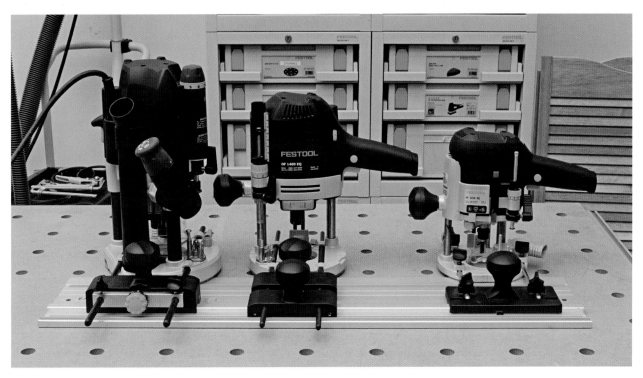

The guide rail works with all three Festool OF routers, left to right the OF 2200, The OF 1400 and the OF 1010.

Both Festool PS jigsaws use the same snap-in plate to connect to the rail system. Both tools are the same power but with different configurations. This is the barrel grip model PS 300.

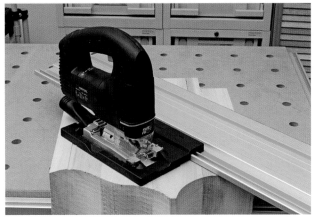

The top handle model is the PSB 300.

Applications of the Guide Rail System

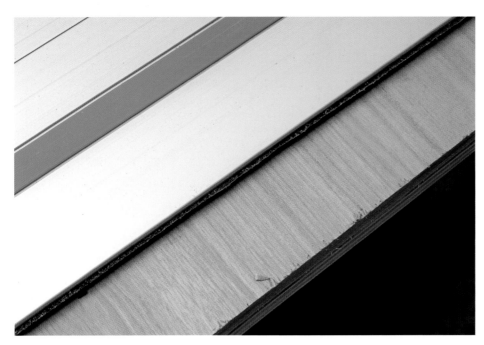

One of the frustrations of most portable circular saws is the difficulty of getting an accurate, straight cut. It involves a complicated alignment procedure, using a typical straight edge, measuring from the blade to the edge of the foot plate, and praying that the edge is straight and the saw doesn't wander away from the line. With the Festool guide rail system everything is made simple. The key to this is the splinter guard is an accurate indicator of the cutting edge and can be aligned directly on the scribe mark. When used with the TS plunge saw, this is true for a beveled cut as well as a straight cut.

Angled Square Cut

Because of the accuracy of the splinterguard, a simple angled square cut can be made by laying the guide rail between two marks.

Suppose an angled cut is needed, going from 30 mm at one edge…

…to 20 mm at the other.

107

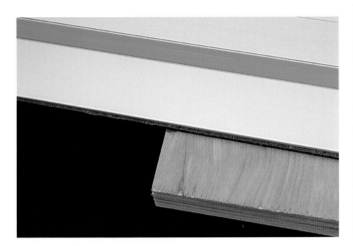

Align the splinter guard on one mark…

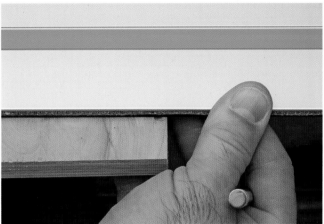

…and the other…

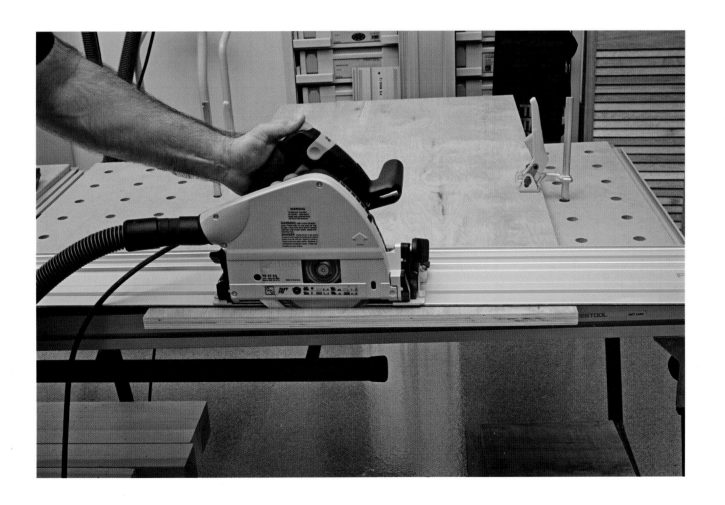

The result is a beautiful, clean cut right to the scribe line.

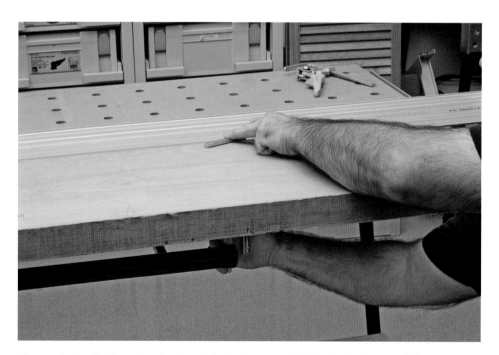

One application for the guide rail system is ripping heavy stock. This often involves special jigs, saws, or, for joining, special planers. With the Festool guide rail system the saw is taken to the wood in a relatively simple procedure. In this example a rip cut is made in an 8 foot piece of 8/4 stock. The piece is first clamped to the table using ratcheting clamps from under the table top. Even with the deep overhang I need, this clamping securely holds the work.

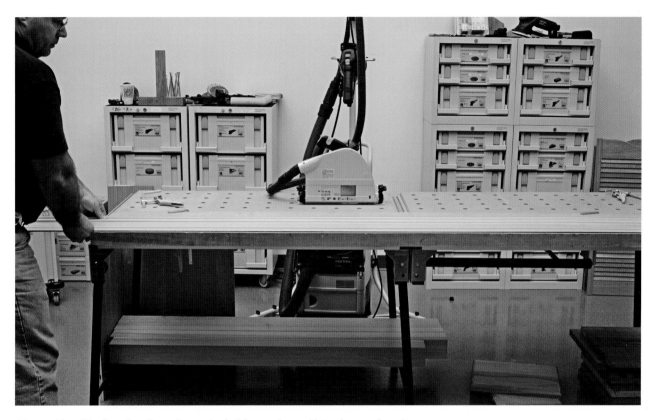

A long guide rail is aligned on the scribe marks. In this case the goal is to clean up the edge.

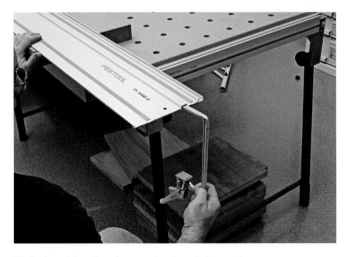

To fix the guide rail to the wood a clamp is inserted into the bottom channel.

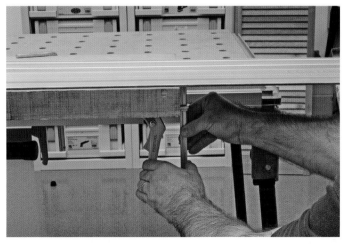

It then slides over to the work piece and is tightened, securely engaging the guide rail. Clamp from both ends.

The TS 75 saw is used on this cut, though the TS 55 could be used with the proper ripping blade. The bigger saw, of course, handles it much more easily. Set the blade depth so it cuts through the stock.

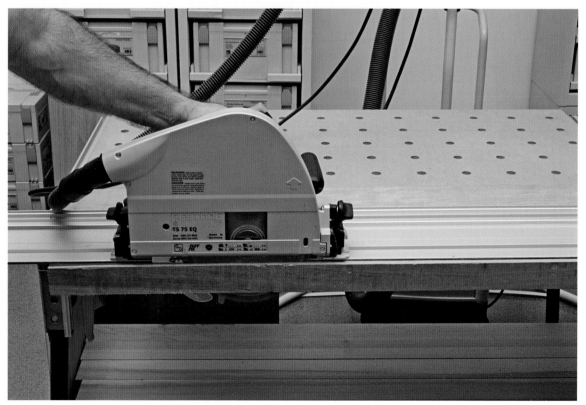

For ripping, plunge the blade before entering the material.

The saw follows the guide all the way through the cut.

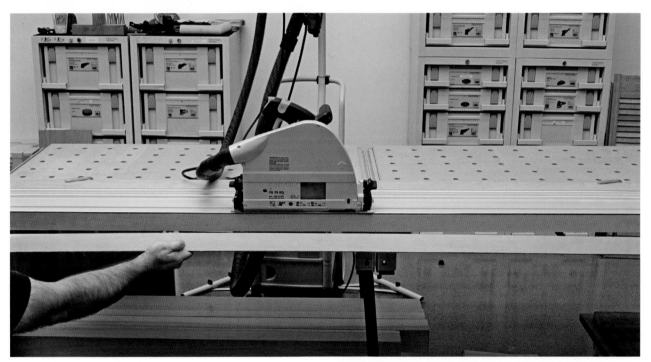

The result, even in this 8/4 cherry board is a finished cut throughout. There is no burning...

...and virtually no saw marks. In short it is a joinable edge, ready for gluing.

5. THE DUST EXTRACTION SYSTEM

Dust control is an integral part of the Festool system and design philosophy. It offers a full line of dust extractors designed to for the workshop or job site, to work with the Festool tools to optimize their operation and effectiveness at the same time as they provide a safe, clean work place.

The cleaning sets come in metal or plastic and the choice of anti-static or non anti-static hoses in three diameters to meet all your tool and dust extraction requirements. A wide assortment of connectors, reducers, and special sleeves allow you to tailor your system.

Festool offers a wide selection of filtration options for ultimate flexibility. In addition to the standard disposable filter bags, Festool offers a long life, re-usable bag. There are four main filters to choose from; standard, long-lasting, wet and HEPA (only available on CT 22 and CT 33). An optional dirt trap is available for wet applications.

Sys-Docks and optional hose hooks, holders and garages (for the CT22 and CT33) are designed for efficient storage of cleaning accessories and Festool Systainers. The flat tops offer added space for tools while you work.

With the optional boom arm, the hoses and cords are kept up and out of the way, opening up the work space.

The CT 22 and CT 33 can be equipped for connecting to pneumatic tools. Compressed air service units, auto-start conversion kits and IAS2 single and double adapters make the CT even more versatile.

Features

• **Tool-triggered activation** for automatic dust extraction.

• **Flat tops with locking latches** to attach Systainers, for ease of transport and storage.

• **Simple, pressure-fit hose connectors** for switching tools quickly.

• **Antistatic hoses are standard** to reduce dust build-up.

• **Ergonomically designed carrying handles and oversized wheels** for ease of movement around the job site.

• **Built-in cord storage** reduces tripping hazards.

• **HEPA filters** eliminate 99.97% of particulates from the air (Only available on CT 22 and CT 33, where they are standard equipment)

• **The motor is completely separate from the dust bin,** significantly prolonging the life of the motor.

• **A**djustable cubic feet per minute (CFM) setting for better results.

Model name	CT MINI	CT MIDI	CT 22 E	CT 33 E
Item	**583 360**	**583 376**	**583 366**	**583 368**
Standard package includes				
Filters	1 micron	1 micron	HEPA	HEPA
Filter bag	2	2	1	1
Antistatic suction hose	1-1/16" x 11.5'	1-1/16" x 11.5'	1-1/16" x 11.5'	1-1/16" x 11.5'
	(27mm x 3.5m)	(27mm x 3.5m)	(27mm x 3.5m)	(27mm x 3.5m)
Container/filter bag capacity	2.6 gal/2 gal	3.96 gal/3.3 gal	5.8 gal/5.3 gal	8.7 gal/7.9 gal
	10 liters/7.5 liters	15 liters/12.5 liters	22 liters/20 liters	33 liters/30 liters
Specifications				
Depth x width x height	17.5" x 13.5" x 16.5"	17.5" x 13.5" x 18.5"	24" x 15" x 17"	24" x 15" x 22"
	(440 x 340 x 420 mm)	(440 x 340 x 470mm)	(625 x 380 x 440 mm)	(625 x 380 x 550 mm)
Weight	21 lbs. (9.5 kg)	21.4 lbs. (9.7 kg)	26.5 lbs. (12 kg)	32 lbs. (14.5 kg)
Noise (sound level)	62 dB (low setting)	62 dB (low setting)	62 dB (low setting)	62 dB (low setting)
	72 dB (maximum setting)	72 dB (max. setting)	72 dB (maximum setting)	72 dB (maximum setting)
Maximum suction capacity	99 CFM	99 CFM	134 CFM	134 CFM
	(2807 l/min)	(2807 l/min)	(3800 l/min)	(3800 l/min)
Maximum vacuum	80" static water lift	80" static water lift	90" static water lift	90" static water lift
	(200000 Pa)	(20000 Pa)	(23000 Pa)	(23000 Pa)
Power consumption	400-1200 watts /	400-1200 watts /	350-1200 watts /	350-1200 watts /
	3.3-10 amps 120 v AC	3.3-10 amps 120 v AC	2.9-10 amps 120 v AC	2.9-10 amps 120 v AC

Left to right: CT Mini (99 cfm, 2 gal. cap.), CT Midi (99 cfm, 3.3 gal. cap.), CT-22 (134 cfm, 5.3 gal cap.), and CT-33 (134 cfm, 7.9 gal. cap.). The smaller two units are great for job sites, being easily portable and small enough to get in tight spots. The CT 33 is mainly a workshop unit, with large capacity and power. The CT 22 is an all purpose unit, with power and size that are good for the shop and job site.

Accessories

Description/Application	Item	Compatibility			
		CT MINI	CT MIDI	CT 22 E	CT 33 E
Hoses—Antistatic					
Antistatic versions are only effective when used with antistatic design (Festool's CT series) dust extractors.					
With rotating connector and reducing sleeve.					
1 1/16" x 11.5' (27 mm x 3.5 m) AS	**452 878**	●	●	●	●
1 1/16" x 16.5' (27 mm x 5 m) AS	**452 880**	●	●	●	●
1 7/16" x 11.5' (36 mm x 3.5 m) AS	**452 882**			●	●
1 7/16" x 16.5' (36 mm x 5 m) AS	**452 884**			●	●
1 7/16" x 23' (36 mm x 7 m) AS	**452 886**			●	●
1 15/16" x 13' (50 mm x 4 m) AS	**452 888**			●	●
1 15/16" x 13' (50 mm x 4 m) AS	**452 890**			●	●
Hoses—Non antistatic					
For use with cleaning sets or non-antistatic dust extractors.					
With rotating connector and reducing sleeve.					
1 1/16" x 11.5' (27 mm x 3.5 m)	**452 877**	●	●	●	●
1 1/16" x 16.5' (27 mm x 5 m)	**452 879**	●	●	●	●
1 15/16" x 11.5' (36 mm x 3.5 m)	**452 881**			●	●
1 15/16" x 16.5' (36 mm x 5 m)	**452 883**			●	●
1 15/16" x 23' (36 mm x 7 m)	**452 885**			●	●
1 15/16" x 8.25' (50 mm x 2.5 m)	**452 887**			●	●
1 15/16" x 13' (50 mm x 4 m)	**452 889**			●	●
Hose Sleeves—Rotating connector					
Hose connector to fit inlet of dust extractor, external dia. 2 9/32" (58 mm).					
Antistatic version for D 50 suction hose	**452 896**			●	●
Antistatic version for D 36 suction hose	**452 894**			●	●
Antistatic version for D 27 suction hose	**452 892**			●	●
Non-antistatic version for D 50 suction hose	**452 895**			●	●
Non-antistatic version for D 36 suction hose	**452 893**			●	●
Non-antistatic version for D 27 suction hose	**452 891**	●	●	●	●
Hose sleeves--Reducing sleeves					
Hose connector for tools or cleaning sets.					
With rotating adapter for D 27 suction hose	**487 071**	●	●	●	●
Replacement. Tool end of extraction hose for our standard 27mm hose.					
Antistatic version with rotating adapter for D 36 suction hose	**487 721**			●	●
Replacement. Tool end of extraction hose for mid-sized 36mm hose.					

Description/Application	Item	Compatibility			
		CT MINI	CT MIDI	CT 22 E	CT 33 E
Non-antistatic hose reducer	452 897			●	●
For reducing from 50mm to 36mm hose or when connecting 36mm to 27mm hose.					
Antistatic angle adapter	456 806	●	●		
Elbow hose end for connection in CT MIDI or CT MINI					
Antistatic connector sleeve	493 047			●	●
To connect suction hoses D 50/D 36/D 27.					
Antistatic Y-piece with blanking plug	452 898			●	●
To connect two suction hoses to the dust extractor.					
Blanking plug	452 899			●	●
For retrofitting on CT 23/33, to seal off inlet during transportation.					
Tubes—Curved					
Stainless steel	452 900	●	●	●	●
To connect tubes to extraction hose for comfortable grip.					
Polypropylene (PP) with air regulating slide to adjust suction power	452 901	●	●	●	●
To connect tubes to extraction hose for comfortable grip.					
Tubes—Extension					
Stainless steel	452 902	●	●	●	●
3 piece, 37 1/2" (950 mm) D 36					
Non-antistatic polypropylene (PP)	452 903	●	●	●	●
3 piece, 37 1/2" (L= 970 mm) D 36					
One-piece anodized aluminum	447 599			●	●
43 1/2" (L= 1100 mm) D 50					
Non-antistatic plastic	440 412			●	●
2-piece, 38" (L= 970 mm) D 50					
Floor nozzles/brushes					
Industrial floor nozzle	452 908	●	●	●	●
High-quality industrial design; aluminum. Width 14 5/8" (370 mm); 2 casters, 2 brush inserts.					
Large Industrial floor nozzle	452 910	●	●	●	●
High-quality industrial design; aluminum.					

Accessories

Description/Application	Item	CT MINI	CT MIDI	CT 22 E	CT 33 E
Width 17 11/16" (450 mm); 2 casters, 2 brush inserts.					
Standard floor nozzle *Plastic. Width 11 13/16" (300 mm) 2 caster, 2 brush inserts*	452 907	●	●	●	●
Workshop floor nozzle *Plastic. Width 14 5/8" (370 mm) 2 caster, 2 brush inserts*	452 909	●	●	●	●
Interchangeable floor nozzle *4-piece, plastic. With 3 replacement inserts (brushes, rubber lips, carpet)*	452 906	●	●	●	●
Multi-purpose floor nozzle *With retractable brush inserts.*	452 911	●	●	●	●
Turbo suction brush *For carpet and hard surface with 4 casters. Width 10 5/8" (270 mm). Suction-activated rolling brushes, requires 36 mm hose.*	450 644			●	●
Special nozzles/brushes					
Suction brush *Plastic, dia. 2 13/16" (70 mm)*	440 404	●	●	●	●
Upholstery brush *Plastic, with brush insert width 4 11/16" (120 mm)*	440 406	●	●	●	●
Universal brush nozzle *Plastic, brush ring 4 11/16" x 1 5/8" (120 x 40 mm)*	440 403	●	●	●	●
Large crevice nozzle *Plastic, length 14 4/8" (370 mm)*	452 912			●	●
Crevice nozzle *Plastic, length 14 5/8" (370 mm)*	452 904	●	●	●	●
Bevel ended nozzle *Flexible rubber, length 7 1/2" (190 mm), outside diameter 1 5/8" (40 mm)*	411 810	●	●	●	●
Other accessories					
Spark trap *For use when operations may generate sparks, i.e. sanding or sawing metal.*	484 733			●	●
Handle *For CT 22 & CT 33 only. Improves mobility. Required for mounting Boom Arm 492 753.*	452 921			●	●
Suction hose holder *Raises hose to table height and prevents trip hazard.*	487 072			●	●
Hose hook *Hose minder for storage or to prevent hose from laying on the ground.*	452 998			●	●

Description/Application	Item	Compatibility			
		CT MINI	CT MIDI	CT 22 E	CT 33 E
Dirt trap	452 925			●	
Collection bucket facilitates disposing of liquids.					
Dirt trap	452 926				●
Collection bucket facilitates disposing of liquids.					
CT adapter plug	493 232	●	●	●	●
Replacement. Adapts the 20 amp CT plug to fit in standard 15 amp outlets.					
Boom arm	492 753			●	●
Keeps the cord and hose up and out of your way; requires handle (SB-CT 452 921) to be mounted onto CT 22/33 dust extractor.					
CT hose garage	494 388			●	●
Stores and protects hose and cord for transport.					
Boom Arm Tool Holder	493 558			●	●
Convenient storage and cradle of two electric sanders. For use with Boom Arm only. Includes wire rack and clamping knob.					
Filter Elements					
Main filter element	452 923			●	●
Standard 1 micron filter replacement-paper. 2 pieces.					
HEPA filter element	493 334			●	●
The highest standard for filtration. Filters particles to .3 microns.					
Wet filter element	454 805	●	●		
Prevents foam buildup associated with wet extraction. 1 piece.					
Wet filter element	452 924			●	●
Prevents foam buildup associated with wet extraction. 2 pieces.					
Longlife filter element	454 869			●	●
Cloth filter with special "M" fold prevents build-up. 2 pieces.					
Filter bags					
Filter bag	456 772	●			
Paper filter bag captures dust. 5 pieces.					
Filter bag	494 105		●		
Paper filter bag captures dust. 5 pieces.					
Filter bag	452 970			●	
Paper filter bag captures dust. Includes dust cap for clean disposal. 5 pieces.					

Accessories

Description/Application	Item	Compatibility			
		CT MINI	CT MIDI	CT 22 E	CT 33 E
Filter bag	**452 971**				●
Paper filter bag captures dust. Includes dust cap for clean disposal. 5 pieces.					
Bulk filter bags 20 *pieces.*	**494 631**			●	
Bulk filter bags 20 *pieces.*	**494 632**				●
Longlife filter bag (re-usable bag)	**456 737**			●	
Economical solution for capturing and eliminating large chips produced by routing or planing. (at least 500 fillings) Re-sealable.					
Longlife filter bag (re-usable bag)	**456 738**				●
Economical solution for capturing and eliminating large chips produced by routing or planing. (at least 500 fillings) Re-sealable.					

The **CT MINI** and **CT MIDI** are Festool's most portable mobile dust extractors. Compact and lightweight, they have enough capacity for common job site tasks. The CT MIDI, somewhat larger in size, offers increased capacity for heavier on-site use. Both units have large wheels and double casters, that can easily negotiate obstacles in the shop or on the job site. Generating 99 CFM of suction, and only 62 dB (on low setting), these CTs can quickly and quietly remove large amounts of debris. One disposable filter comes standard on the CT MINI and CT MIDI, with the option of additional dry and wet filters to meet your every need. The integrated hose garage keeps hoses and cords well organized and makes Systainer transport simple and efficient.

CT Mini & CT Midi Features:

• **Integrated Sys-Dock and hose garage.** Cords and hoses conveniently store in the onboard hose garage, while the flat top and locking latches allow you to attach one or more Systainers.

• **Filter bag.** Disposable, two-ply filter bags are particularly tear-resistant; an integrated dust cap prevents dust from spilling during disposal.

• **Tool-less main filter and automatic water level detector.** The main filter can be changed without using tools. The internal sensors monitor the fluid level, for wet applications, and switch the mobile dust extractor off automatically when the container is full.

• **Automatic tool start/Adjustable suction.** Smooth start, infinitely adjustable electronic air flow control and tool-triggered or manual on-off switch ensures convenient and efficient dust control.

• **Convenient carry handle.** The ergonomic handle makes maneuvering these small and light dust extractors a breeze.

• **Foot brake.** Quick on/off foot actuated brake prevents roll-off during usage or during transport.

• **Anti-static hose.** A 1" x 11.5' (27mm x 3.5m) anti-static hose comes standard.

• **Large wheels.** Large wheels, low center of gravity, and ergonomically balanced design allows you to move the CT effortlessly around the job site.

• **Mobility.** The manageable size makes it easy to transport or carry up stairs.

The CT MINI (left) and CT MIDI (right) are nearly identical machines, except for the larger capacity of the MIDI.

Foot brake. When pushed all the way down, it raises the wheels off the ground and keeps the unit in place. This is useful during transport of the unit and on the job site.

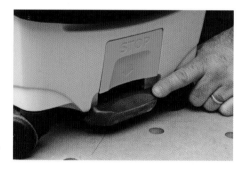

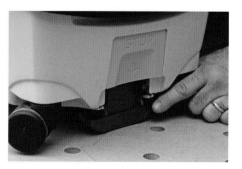

The 27 mm anti-static hose does not allow dust to cling during use. When the vac is turned off, there is no dust in the hose to fall back into the workspace.

Variable suction control. This is especially important during sanding operations, where a powerful suction could pull the pad too snugly against the work. This would create excessive friction and heat, making swirl marks on the material. By lowering the suction to the correct level, the sanding proceeds much more smoothly and cleanly.

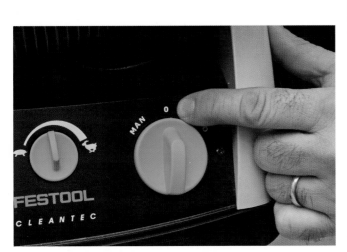

ON/OFF switch. "0" equals off.

"MAN" is manual, turning the vac on.

The CT MINI & MIDI

"AUTO" is automatic, meaning that the vac is turned on when the tool is on.

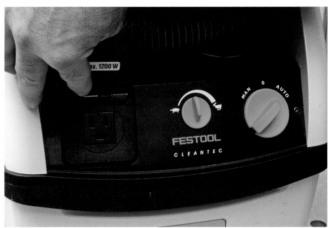

The AUTO function works when the tool is plugged into this outlet on the vac.

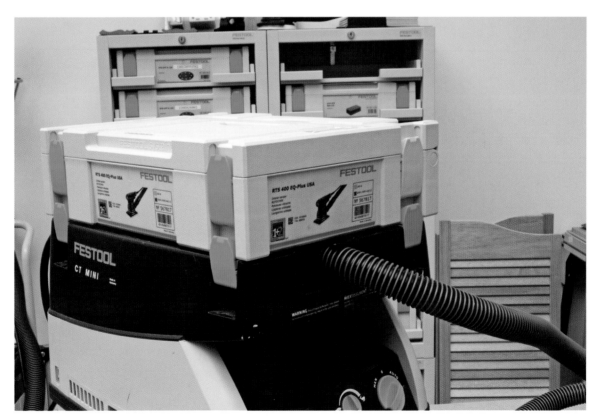

The SYS-DOCK allows various SYSTAINERS to be securely attached to the top of the vac for easy transport…the vac actual serves as a dolly.

There are four latches for the SYS-DOCK, one at the front and back, and two on one side. With the SYSTAINER in place, open the latch, pull it up and lock it in place.

To gain access to the bag and filters, undo the latches on both sides of the base.

Lift the top by the handle.

The CT MINI & MIDI

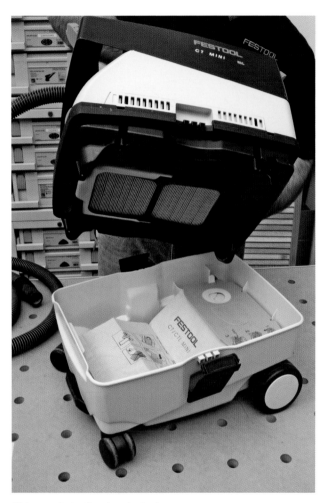

This reveals the filter bag, in the bottom compartment, and the filters under the lid.

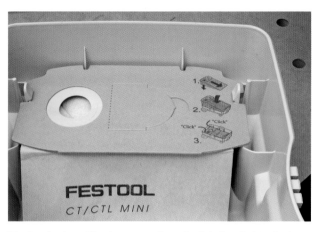

The bag in place. The dust comes from the job directly into the bag. Particles 5 microns or greater stay there. The smaller bits move through the bag into the filter, which captures particles 1 micron in size or larger.

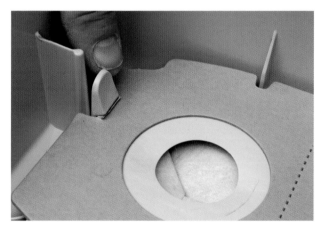

Clips on either side hold the bag in place.

When the bag is full this tab is lifted…

…and pressed in place to seal the bag, keeping the dust inside.

The 1 micron filter.

For cleaning, pull the handle out…

…and remove the filter.

To clean, remove the filter from the frame…

…and tap against the side of a trash can. Used properly the filters will last a very long time. Replace when there is a noticeable loss of air flow, even after replacing the bag and cleaning the air filter.

Extra filter bags can be stored in this space at the back.

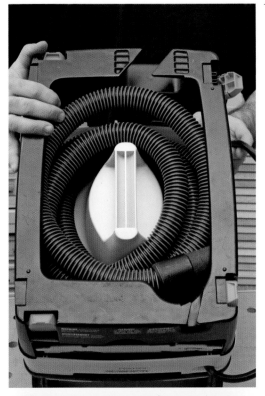

The hose and cord are neatly stored in the top.

The vacs come with a 20 amp plug to go into 20 amp outlets, now required in most commercial applications.

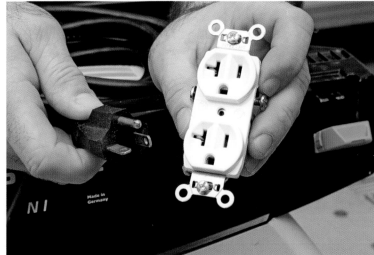

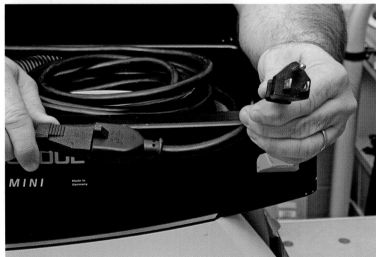

Since most residences and older construction do not have these outlets, there is a 15 amp plug adapter available. These are easily lost, so it is best to have a few in your toolbox.

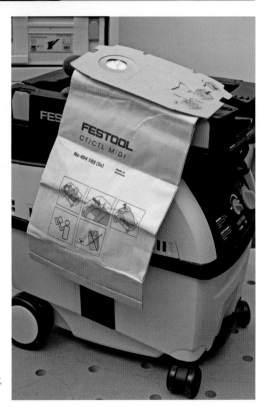

The CT MIDI bag has a 3.3 gallon dry capacity, about 1.3 gallons more than the CT MINI.

Converting the CT MINI & MIDI
for Wet Vacuuming

For wet vac use, the filter can be replaced with a foam breaking wet filter element.

Remove the bag.

Remove the 1 micron filter...

...and replace with the foam breaking filter.

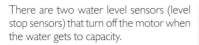

There are two water level sensors (level stop sensors) that turn off the motor when the water gets to capacity.

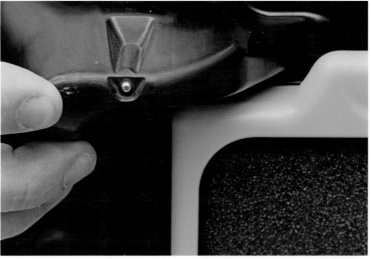

CT 22 E & CT 33 E

The **CT 22 E** and **CT 33 E** are Festool's most powerful mobile dust extractors. With a sturdy chassis, extra large wheels, and double casters, these units can easily negotiate obstacles in the shop or on the job site. With 134 CFM and only 62 db (on the low setting), these CTs can quickly and quietly remove large amounts of debris, with minimal noise distractions. HEPA filters come standard on the CT 22 E and CT 33 E and offer the ultimate in clean air and filtration. Integrated Sys-Docks or the optional hose garage allow you to attach one or more Systainers for added convenience. An optional boom arm makes a perfect companion in a shop environment and keeps hoses and cords organized and away from work surfaces.

CT 22 E & CT 33 E Features

• **Bypass blower port.** The bypass blower port allows you to evacuate unpleasant odors and fumes from the job site, by attaching an additional hose.

• **HEPA filters.** HEPA filters are standard and remove 99.97% of particulate to .3 micron.

• **Automatic tool start and adjustable suction.** Smooth start, infinitely adjustable electronic air flow control and tool-triggered or manual on-off switch ensures convenient and efficient dust control.

• **Convenient carry handle.** Ergonomic handle is positioned 7-9 inches in from the body, which is the most natural position for lifting.

• **Filter scrubber.** The convenient scrubber handle removes the accumulation of dust and debris on the internal filter, without the need to open the machine and improves air circulation across the motor.

• **Sys-Dock and anti-static hose.** The flat top with locking latches allows you to transport tools and accessories securely and conveniently when used with a Festool Systainer. As with all CT dust extractors, the 1-1/16" x 11.5' (27mm x 3.5m) anti-static hose comes standard.

• **Automatic water level sensor and optional dirt trap.** With wet applications, the internal sensors monitor the fluid level and switches the mobile dust extractor off when the container is full (dirt trap available as an accessory).

• **Cord storage.** Everything needs its own storage space. The cord can be wound on the dedicated cord wrap to prevent it from getting in the way during transportation.

• **Tool-less filter changes.** If there is ever a need to change filters, or if you want to switch to a sponge filter for wet applications, changing the filter is very easy. The flat filter can be changed without using tools.

The CT 33 E is nearly identical to the CT 22 E with the exception of capacity.
The CT 33 E holds 2.6 gallons more than the CT 22 E.

The CT 33 E has a small storage compartment in front, useful for spare bags.

The controls are the same as the smaller units…

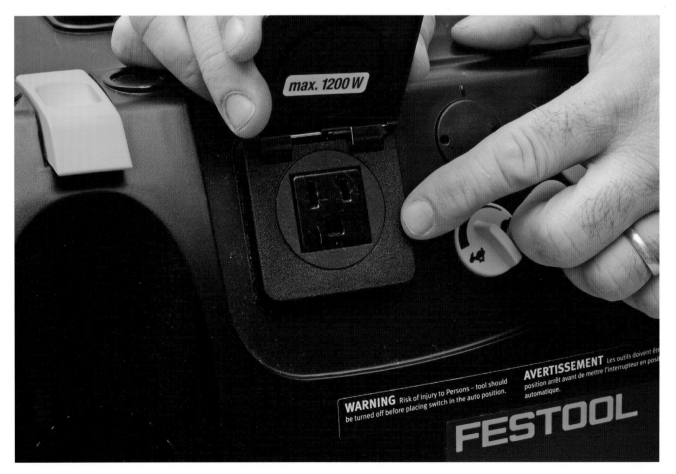

…with the tool outlet behind the door.

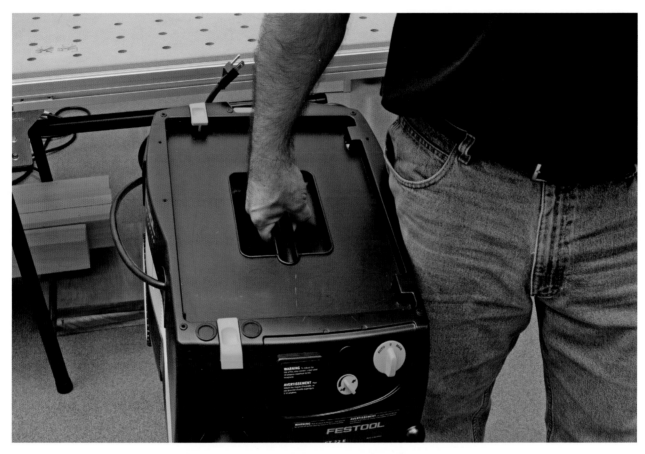

The handle is ergonomically designed to be about 7-9 inches from the body, a comfortable carrying position.

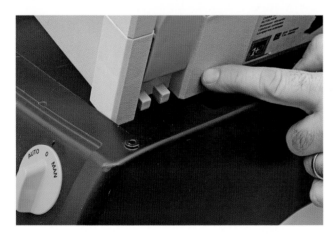

The Sys-Dock system is somewhat different. Tabs at the lower edge of the Systainer…

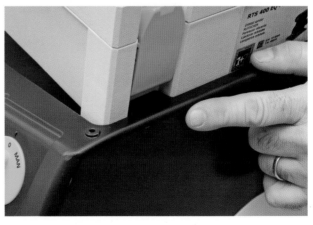

…fit into sockets on the inner edge of the top of the vac.

Lower the Systainer into place and latch it at the opposite side.

The latch simply slides into place.

Large, non-marring wheels on this unit allow for easy movement.

Wheel locks are located inside the rear wheels. Simply push them down to engage the lock.

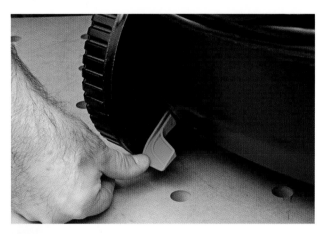

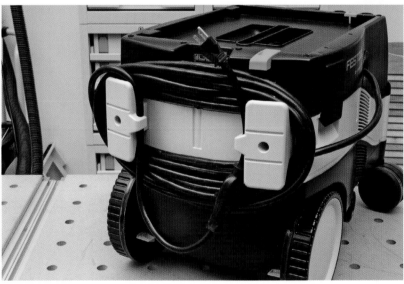

The cord is stored on the rear.

On the side are the exhaust ports. This grille is the normal exhaust outlet.

Beneath it is the round exhaust port that allows venting to the outside, removing any odors or vapors that are not captured by the HEPA filter. There is a flap inside that raises when the hose is inserted, blocking the normal venting system.

The exhaust hose can be run to a place outside the work area.

The green handle at the back of the unit operates the quick filter scrubber. Pull it in and out a couple of times while the unit is off and it knocks the dust into the reservoir. This will prevent the filters from caking. A thorough cleaning is done by removing the filters and tapping them.

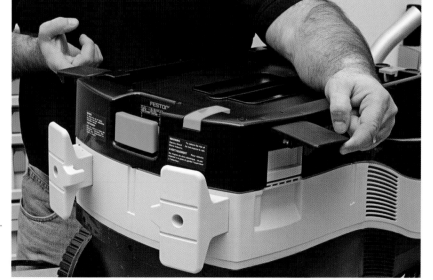

To access the bag and filters, lift the release latches on both sides.

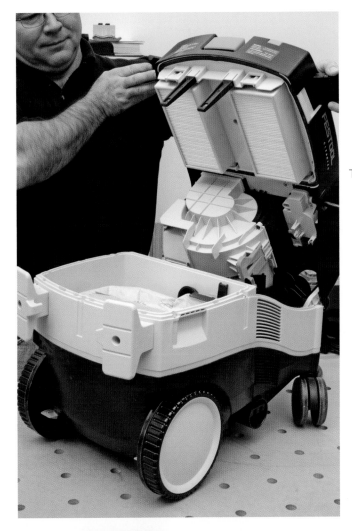

The lids lifts from the back.

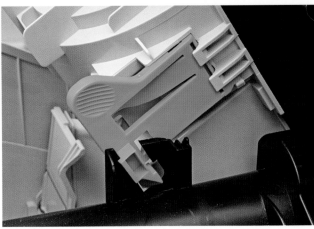

A kickstand automatically engages to keep the lid up.

To release the kickstand, simple press in the tab.

The 5 micron bag fits in the well.

To remove it, pull back on the tab at the opening.

Insert the cap to seal the bag.

Insert a new bag, using your hand to keep it straight.

When it is snuggly in place, bend the tab down. This promotes uniform filling and prevents tearing when removing the bag.

This is the grounding contact for the hose. The grounding strap allows the unit to have continuity for the anti-static hose design and ground the intake port to the electrical ground.

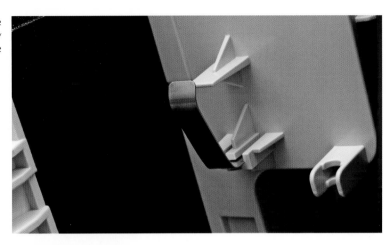

The latch for the HEPA filter.

Depress the latch and pull down the filter frame.

When the frame is free from the unit, the filter simply pops out.

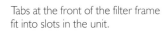
Tabs at the front of the filter frame fit into slots in the unit.

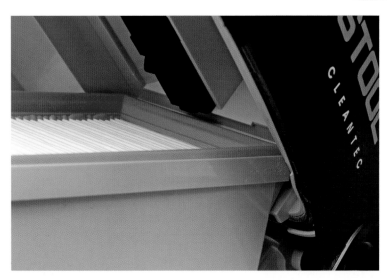

Insert them and pivot the frame into position. The black apparatus above the filter tray is the quick filter scrubber.

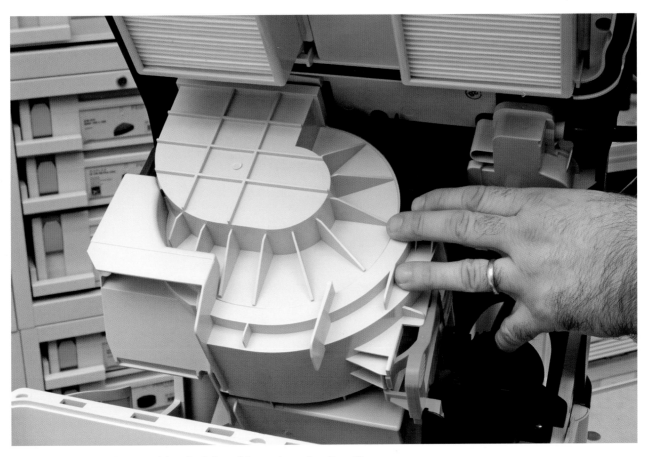

The motor is completely encased, keeping it free of dust and ensuring a long life.

In wet vac mode, the level stop sensors turn the
motor off when the reservoir is filled.

Wet Vacuuming with the CT 22 E & CT 33 E

To convert to wet vac mode, remove the bag.

Remove paper filter…

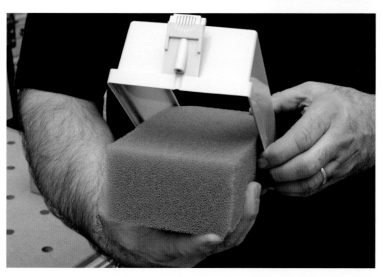

…and replace with foam-breaking wet filter element.

Reinsert the filter frames.

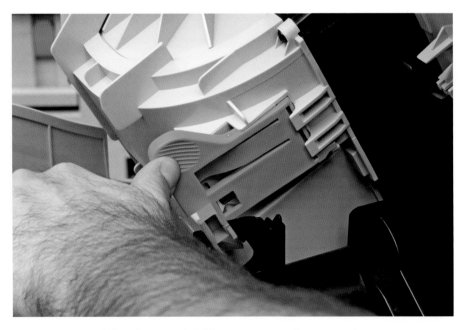

When the reservoir is full you can remove the top to make
emptying it easier. Release the green kickstand.

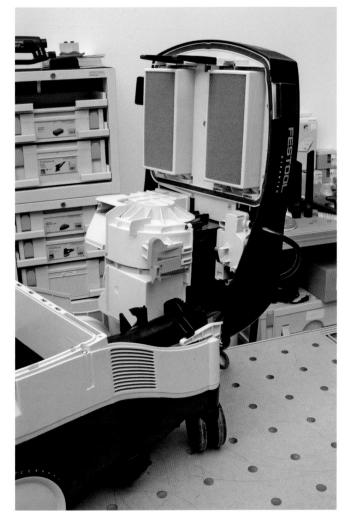

Pivot the top to the vertical position.

Pull the top straight out.

There is a handle at the front end…

...which makes emptying quite easy.

Reinsert the top. The long piece on the left goes above and the smaller rounder tab gets inserted into the slot.

Progress

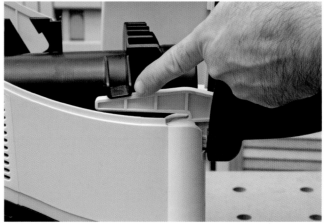

In place.

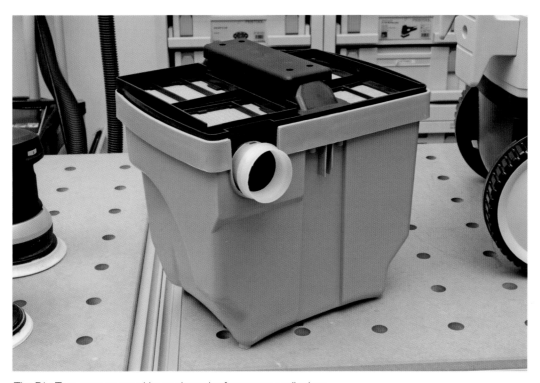

The Dirt Trap accessory provides an alternative for wet vac applications.

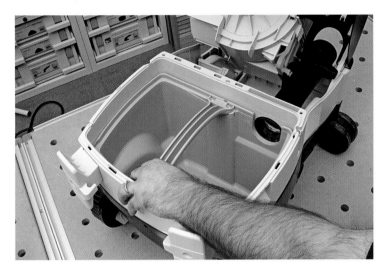

Insert the pail into the well.

The dirt screen then fits on top. Align the input in the hole…

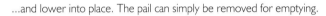

…and lower into place. The pail can simply be removed for emptying.

Hoses

The standard hose for all dust extractors is antistatic, 27mm (1-1/16 inch) diameter, 3.5 meter (11.5 feet) long. This coordinates with the standard tool power cord, which is 13 feet long. It is also available in lengths up to 16.5 feet, which would require an extension cord.

A 36mm (1-7/16 inch) antistatic hose is available for the CT 22 E and CT 33 E. This will prevent clogging when using tools that produce larger chips and sawdust quickly, like a router or planer. Available in lengths of 11.5 feet, 16.5, and 23 feet.

The dust shrouds of the tools are designed to fit with both the 27mm and the 36mm hoses. On the 27mm, the hose fits in the shroud.

On the 36mm, the shroud fits in the hose.

Hoses

The largest antistatic hose is 50mm (2-inches). It is offered in 8.25 and 13 feet. Its main purposes are to connect the dust extractor to shop tools and for shop clean-up.

All the hoses just discussed are available as non-antistatic, "gray" hose. This is good for the exhaust feature on the CT 22 E and CT 33 E, and for connection to a dust extractor by other manufacturers that do not offer the antistatic feature.

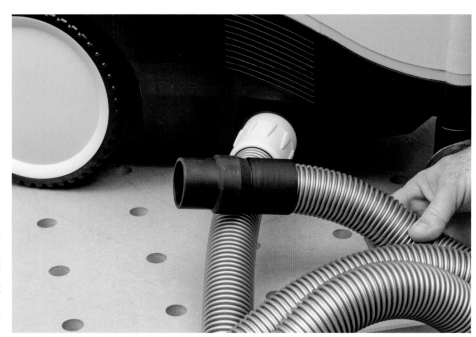

The Y-piece, allows the dust extractor to be connected to two devices. It plugs into the extractor, and has a blanking plug to close one of the branches when not in use.

Sometimes it is necessary to extend the hose. The combination depends on the application. In this case a 36mm hose from the extractor, on the right, is connecting to a 27mm hose going to the tool, on the left.

Connectors for the CT 22 E and CT 33 E

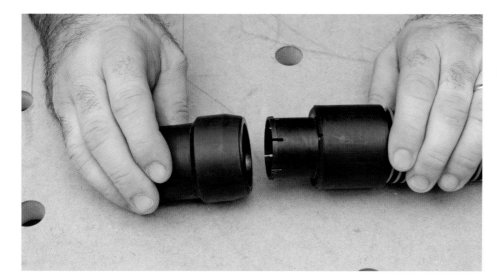

First, pull off the collar.

Then, unscrew the 36mm rotating connector collar. It follows the ribs in the hose, so it unscrews in a clockwise direction.

The rotating connector comes in antistatic and non-antistatic varieties. It has three parts as shown here. Left to right: rotating hose connector, threaded hose sleeve, and hose connector clip.

Place the clip around the hose.

Screw the hose sleeve onto the hose, turning it counterclockwise.

Clip the rotating connector in place.

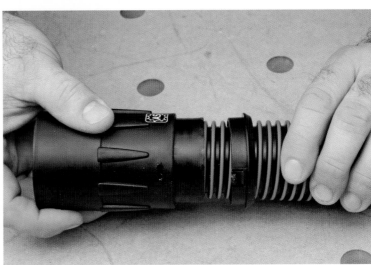

Connectors for the CT 22 E and CT 33 E

Complete.

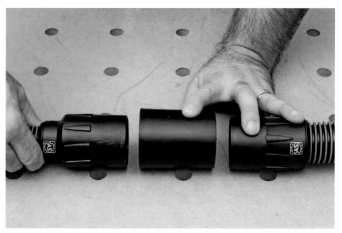

The two hoses can now be joined with the connector sleeve or to a hose reducer coupling sleeve as needed.

Connectors, left to right: Antistatic connector sleeve; antistatic rotating connector sleeve for 27mm suction hose; antistatic rotating connector sleeve for 36mm suction hose; antistatic rotating connector sleeve for 50mm suction hose.

A blanking plug can be used to seal the intake hole in the dust extractor. The pointed tail…

…fits into a slot beneath the hole.

This is a convenient accessory for keeping the dust from escaping during transport.

The spark trap can be added to the system and is vital when working with metal. The baffled chamber cools down the metal particulate before it hits the bag. It helps to reduce the chance of fire from stray sparks while maintaining air flow.

The hose holder is inserted into the accessory socket at the upper front corner.

The hose holder gets the hose up and level with the work area.

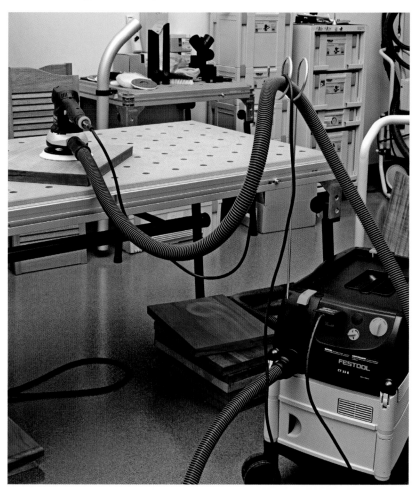

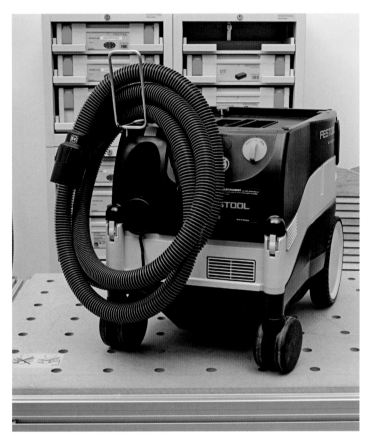

Alternatively, the hose hook fits on the front on the CT22 or CT33, with the rod inserted in the socket at the front corner, and a screw holding it in place. It provides convenient hose storage.

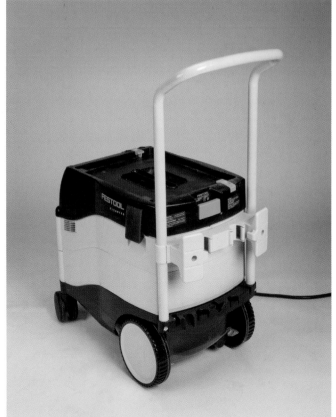

The optional handle assembly makes moving the CT 22 E or CT 33 E even easier. With it the unit can be pushed while standing as opposed to leaning over or carrying. When transporting several Systainers on the Sys-Dock feature, the handle converts the CT into a useful "dolly."

The installation of the optional handle begins with the removal of the cord holders from the back of the machine.

Install the bottom handle assembly…

…and the upper handle assembly.

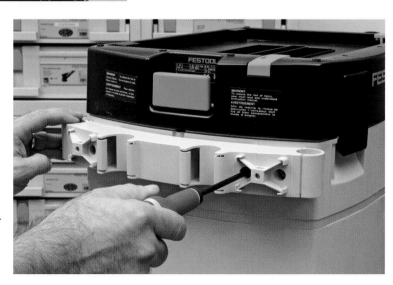

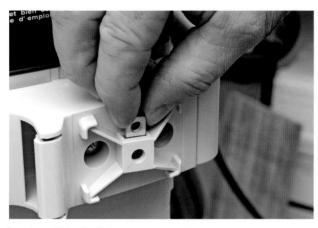

Insert a nut into the slot.

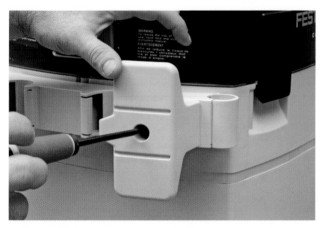

Reinstall the cord holders.

...and secure.

Insert the handle...

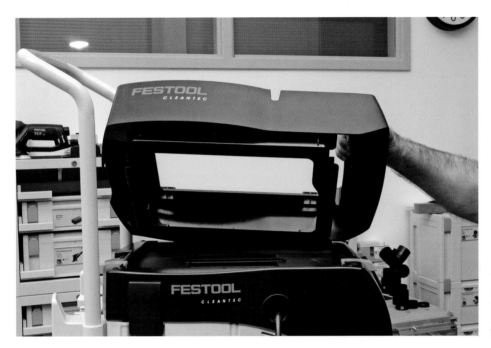

The CT hose garage fits on the top and provides convenient storage space for the hose and cord. Set it in place, with tabs in the slots along the left side…

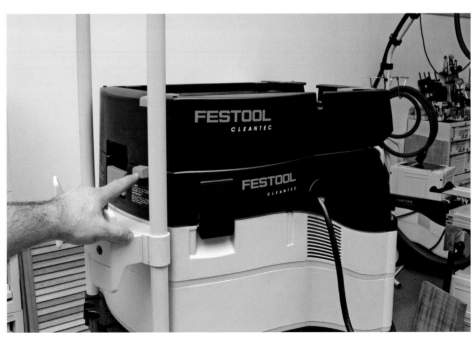

…and lock it.

The Longlife filter bag provides a reusable alternative to paper.

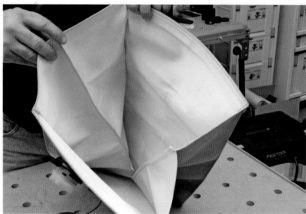

It is lined with fabric for fine filtration.

It closes with this slider.

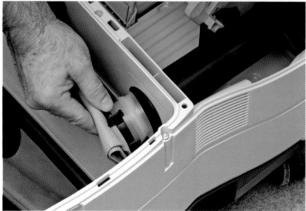

Place the bag in the well and connect
to the dust extraction tube.

The Boom Arm for the CT 22 E and CT 33 E

The Boom Arm accessory keeps the dust extractor hose accessible to the work area, while lifting it up and out of the way of the work at hand. The pivoting arm moves with the tool so it doesn't hinder the work process. It works with the CT 22 E and the CT 33 E and requires the handle assembly. The boom arm comes with a 50mm antistatic extension hose and 3-wire 12 gauge extension power cord. It will accommodate a 27mm or 36mm tool hose, as well as the Festool pneumatic 3-in-1 hose for air tools.

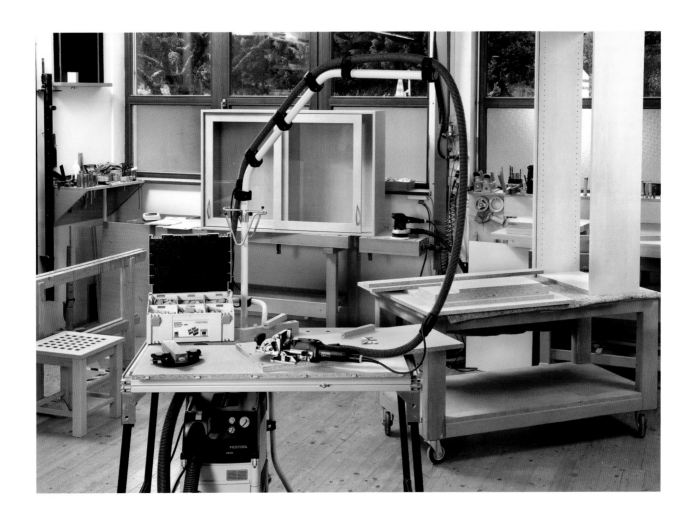

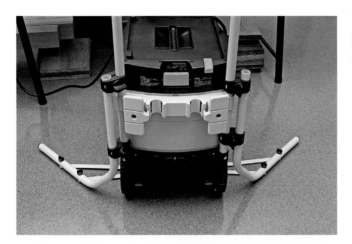

The boom arm requires the handle assembly to be in place. Attaching the boom begins with the outriggers, two added feet that give the unit stability. They are attached to the handles with two tool clamps on each side.

Cross braces give the outriggers added rigidity. Note: This configuration is good if you tend to run the dust extractor from the front of the machine. If you work more from the back the outriggers can be reversed.

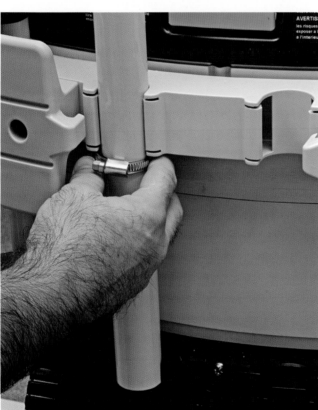

The vertical fits on the lower handle bracket, where a tab keeps it from turning. It then fits in the upper handle support, where a screw clamp underneath, keeps it from riding up.

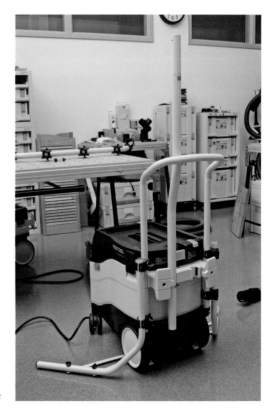

The vertical piece in place

The Boom Arm for the CT 22 E and CT 33 E

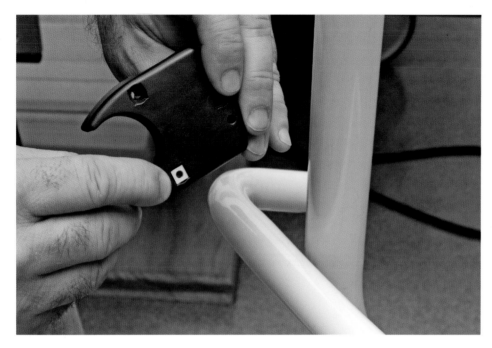

The vertical support is held to the handle with a clamp. The underside holds three recessed nuts.

Place the bottom piece around the vertical support and under the handle.

Place the top piece in position.

Hold it in place with three bolts.

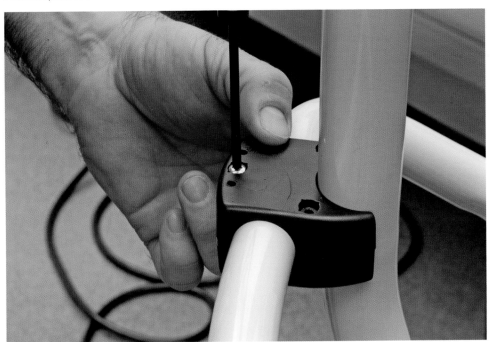

The Boom Arm for the CT 22 E and CT 33 E

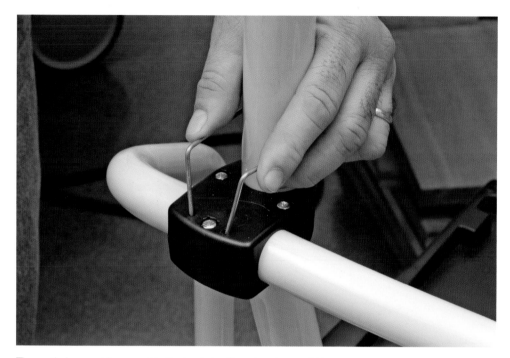

The vertical support is secured to the bracket with a wire clamp, which is inserted into two holes at the back of the bracket.

In place.

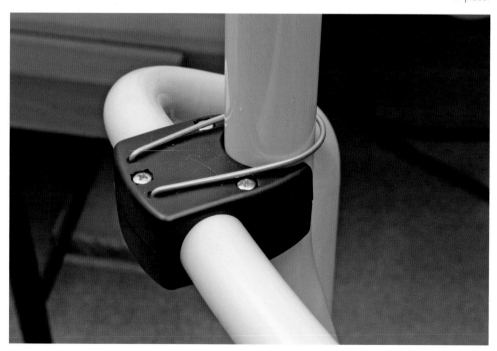

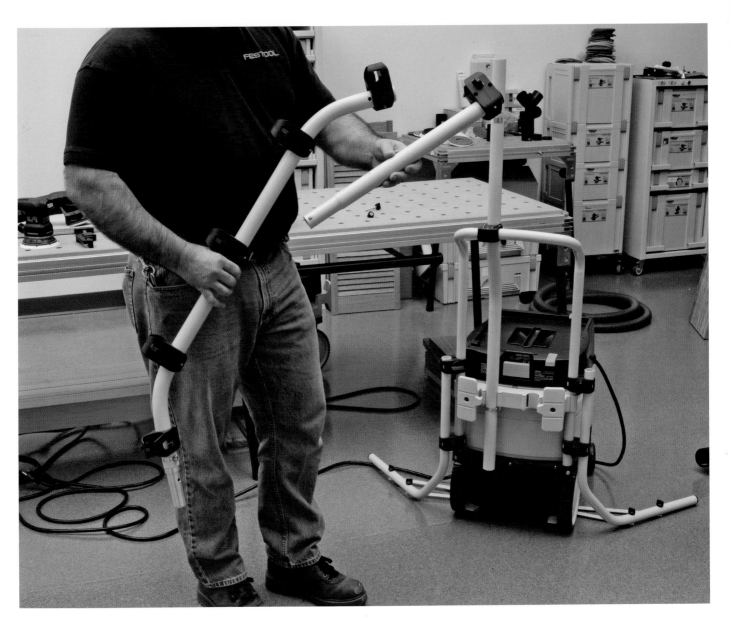

The arm arrives in two segments.

Snap them together.

Insert the arm into the vertical support.

Secure with the bolt provided.

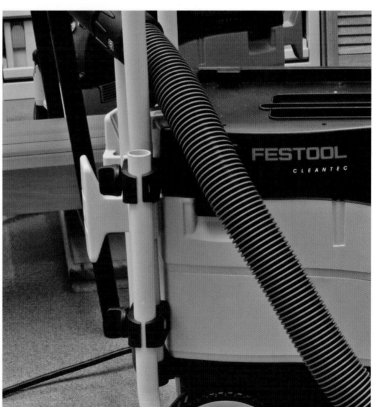

Ready for installation of the
hose and power cord.

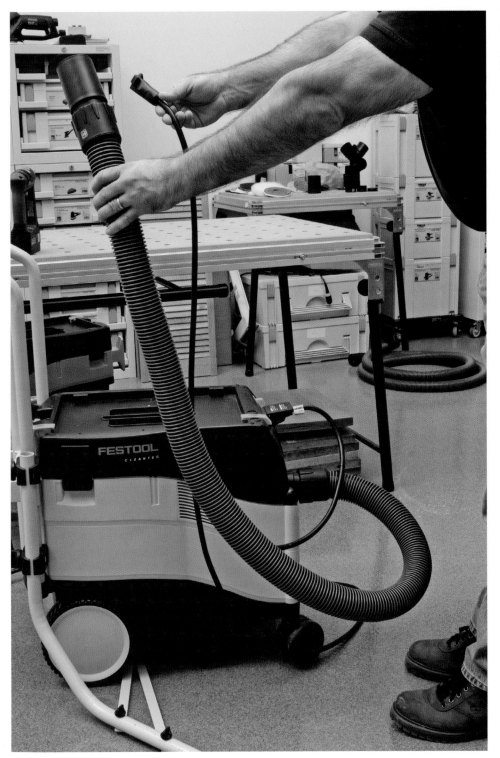

The arm comes with a 50mm antistatic extension hose and 3-wire 12 gauge extension power cord, that run from the extractor to the boom arm.

The Boom Arm for the CT 22 E and CT 33 E

The arm will accommodate a 27mm or 36mm tool hose, as well as the Festool pneumatic 3-in-1 hose for air tools. Insert it in the hose brackets, starting where the arm joins the hose coming off the dust extractor.

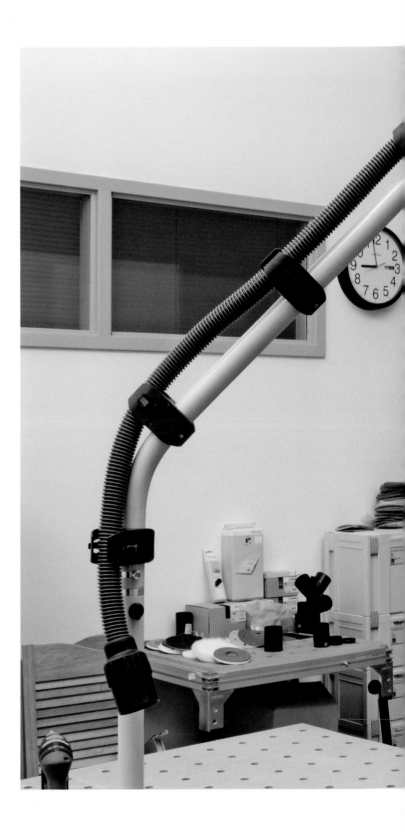

Continue to the end of the arm

The Boom Arm for the CT 22 E and CT 33 E

The tool's power cord is clamped to the outside of the hose brackets.

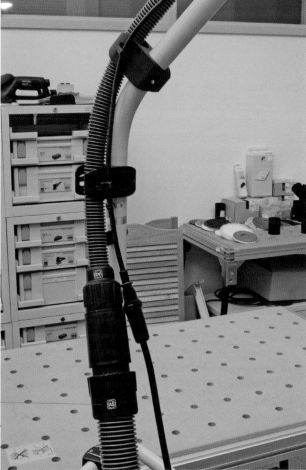

Connect the power cords and hoses.

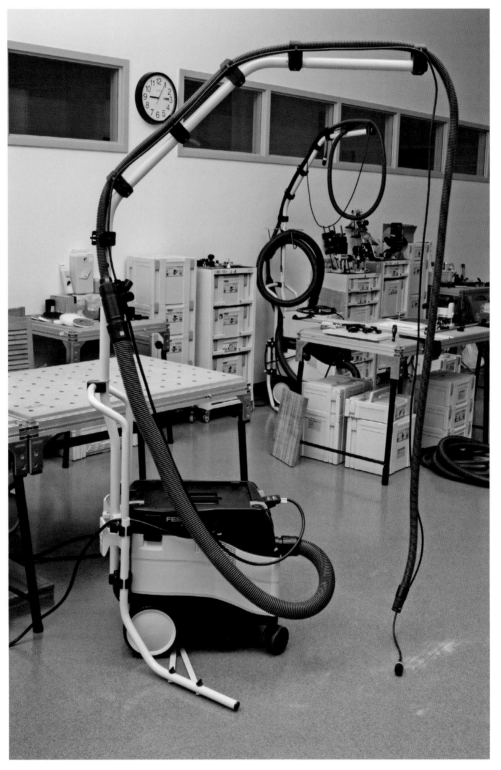

Complete

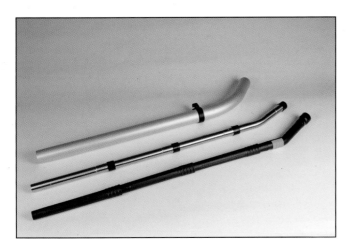

Top to bottom: one-piece anodized aluminum tub; stainless steel curved tube and extensions; curved polyproplyene (PP) curved tube with regulating slide to adjust suction power.

Nozzles & brushes (left to right): Large crevice nozzle; crevice nozzle; universal brush nozzle; upholstery brush; bevel ended nozzle; suction brush.

Floor nozzles (front row, left to right): Large industrial floor nozzle; industrial floor nozzle; interchangeable floor nozzle; (back row, left to right): turbo suction brush; multi-purpose floor nozzle; workshop floor nozzle; standard floor nozzle.